International Learning and International Education in a Global Age

Richard C. Remy
James A. Nathan
James M. Becker
Judith V. Torney

Bulletin 47

Published by
THE NATIONAL COUNCIL FOR THE SOCIAL STUDIES
as a cooperative venture with
The American Political Science Association's
Committee on Pre-Collegiate Education

NATIONAL COUNCIL FOR THE SOCIAL STUDIES

Officers for 1975

President
  Jean Tilford
  Cincinnati (Ohio)
  Public Schools

President-Elect
  James P. Shaver
  Utah State University
  Logan, Utah

Vice-President
  Howard D. Mehlinger
  Indiana University
  Bloomington, Indiana

Executive Director
  Brian J. Larkin
  Washington, D.C.

Editor
  Daniel Roselle
  Washington, D.C.

Executive Secretary Emeritus
  Merrill F. Hartshorn
  Washington, D.C.

Directors
  Harris L. Dante
  Jean Fair
  Paul Flaum
  Gail R. Kirk
  Pauline Kouris
  W. Jerry Larkin
  Charles L. Mitsakos
  Jane Lowrie Mounts
  Raymond H. Muessig
  Anna S. Ochoa
  Helen F. Rogers
  Seymour B. Stiss
  Stanley P. Wronski
  Carolyn Keith, *Ex Officio*

Publications Board
  Nancy Sprague, *Chairperson*
  James A. Banks
  R. Beery
  Barry K. Beyer
  Celeste P. Woodley

JAMES A. BANKS, Publications Board Coordinator for
International Learning and International Education in a Global Age

The NATIONAL COUNCIL FOR THE SOCIAL STUDIES is the professional organization of educators at all levels—elementary, secondary, college and university—who are interested in the teaching of social studies. Membership in the NATIONAL COUNCIL FOR THE SOCIAL STUDIES includes a subscription to the Council's official journal, *Social Education*, a copy of the Yearbook, and a periodic newsletter. In addition, the Council publishes bulletins, curriculum studies, pamphlets, and other materials of practical use for teachers of the social studies. Membership dues are $15.00 a year. Applications for membership and orders for the purchase of publications should be sent to the Executive Director, 1201 Sixteenth Street, N.W., Washington D.C. 20036.

Copyright © 1975 by the
NATIONAL COUNCIL FOR THE SOCIAL STUDIES
Library of Congress Catalog Card Number: 75-7588

Acknowledgements

Several people deserve recognition for their contributions to the development of this volume. Lee Anderson, Richard C. Snyder and Merrill Hartshorn initiated the project as part of a larger effort to build collaborative relationships between the National Council for the Social Studies and the American Political Science Association.

The American Political Science Association's Committee on Pre-Collegiate Education and Political Science Education Project provided the resources and opportunity to collect and review the pertinent research literature.

Anna S. Ochoa consistently encouraged and supported the project. James A. Banks and Nancy Sprague coordinated a review process which yielded many helpful suggestions. Regis Birckbichler of Westerville High School offered a thoughtful critique of the manuscript. Judy Kies, of the Mershon Center, provided invaluable editorial assistance.

Sandy Conyers, Molly Waddill and Rachel Matalon did an excellent job of typing the manuscript.

Finally, we are grateful to the Mershon Center at Ohio State University for providing conditions which facilitated the completion of the manuscript.

Preface

Our goal in writing this volume has been to provide information about international learning and international scholarship which can contribute to improved instruction about the global dimensions of human affairs. In what follows we try to present the research findings on pre-adult political learning in a concise fashion; we attempt to delineate alternative frameworks for viewing the world in a way which will assist educators in becoming more self-conscious about the images of the world which underlie their teaching; and we seek to consider the implication of current scholarship for designing world studies programs. We hope our work contributes to a revitalization of the international dimension of political education.

RICHARD C. REMY
JAMES A. NATHAN
JAMES M. BECKER
JUDITH V. TORNEY

Foreword

The crack of an assassin's pistol anywhere in the world can be brought to the attention of every interested citizen within minutes. But, the capacity of the average citizen to select, analyze, and pass judgment upon that news has not expanded in proportion to the extraordinary increase of information. In this situation, knowledge often spells bewilderment.

In the present age of outstanding technical development, there is a mounting disparity between the limitless capacity of the machines and the limited faculties of their human managers. Most thoughtful observers of the world agree that war and poverty remain the truly desperate enigmas confronting the world today. Solutions can only be reached by the creation of a more enlightened citizenry which can convert fear to fair-mindedness and rational greed to international cooperation. Then, there will be hope for peace and a future for humanity.

Social studies teachers know that, while it is essential to provide sufficient and accurate information about the world and its interactions, this approach alone is not sufficient to bring those understandings, attitudes, and skills so necessary to create an informed citizenry capable of sustaining a constructive and humane global environment. A fresh look at this whole milieu has been long overdue.

International Learning and International Education in a Global Age does this. It is not just another series of pages about international education filled with patterned phrases which result in a newly camouflaged receptacle for bits of educational jargon. It is a stimulating statement about learning to live effectively in a global age. Realistically, it investigates the ways in which productive international education can be accomplished. The Introduction to the volume deserves particular attention for its forceful statement of the rationale.

The Council is particularly indebted to Richard C. Remy, James A. Nathan, James M. Becker, and Judith V. Torney for their perceptive scholarship in the arena of international learning and international education.

The National Council for the Social Studies is pleased to present this publication to the reader as an important addition to the literature of social studies education.

JEAN TILFORD, *President*
National Council for the Social Studies

Contents

PREFACE iv

FOREWORD by *Jean Tilford* v

CHAPTER 1: Introduction 1

CHAPTER 2: Learning about the World 5

Research on Political Learning   8

Learning about the World during
Childhood and Adolescence   10

     Development of a Sense of National Identity   10

     Orientations toward Other Nations and Peoples   12

     Orientations toward the United Nations   18

     Orientations toward the United States as an
     International Actor   23

     Orientations toward War and Peace   28

     Orientations toward the Future of
     International Society   34

     Sources of Information about the
     International System   37

Conclusion   39

CHAPTER 3: Alternative Views of the World 45

The State-Centric View of the World	46
Alternatives to the State-Centric View	48
The Global System View of the World	50
The Moral Unity of the Human Race: A View of the World	53
Implications of Alternative Views for International Education	54
The State-Centric View in the Classroom	55
The Global System and the Moral Unity of the Human Race in the Classroom	57
The Moral Unity of the Human Race	58
The Global System	59
Conclusion	64

CHAPTER 4: Designing World Studies Programs 69

Goals and Motivations	70
Checking Student Views	72
Teacher Preferences	73
Educators and the World of Scholarship	74
Media and International Studies	74
Cross-cultural Training and Experience	76

Appendix 85

Part I A World Studies Bibliography	87
A. Background Reading and Sources of Materials for Teachers	87
B. Ideas and Materials for Use in the Classroom	91
Part II Guidelines for World Studies	93
A. Guidelines and Checklist for World Studies	93
B. Guidelines for World Studies: Suggested Topics, Content, and Evaluation of Present Program	98
C. Guidelines for Selecting World Studies Materials	100

About the Authors

RICHARD C. REMY is Director of Mershon Center's Political Education Program at Ohio State University. He is a political scientist with special interests in the area of political education and political socialization.

JAMES A. NATHAN is an Assistant Professor of Political Science at the University of Delaware. He is a specialist in the field of international relations and foreign policy.

JAMES M. BECKER is Director of the Social Studies Diffusion Project at Indiana University and President of the Mid-America Center for Global Perspectives in Education. He is a specialist in the diffusion of educational innovations and in international education.

JUDITH V. TORNEY is an Associate Professor in the Department of Psychology and College of Education at the University of Illinois at Chicago Circle. She has special interests in cross-national research on children's political learning.

CHAPTER 1

Introduction

Change is part of the human condition. Several interrelated changes with implications for those interested in international education have prompted us to write this book. First, the world is changing. We are currently experiencing the globalization of the human condition. Fundamental changes which make today's world qualitatively different from yesterday's include the spread of atomic weapons to many nations, the worldwide growth of literacy, the development of a global electronic communications network, the emergence of a truly global cultural milieu and economy, and the expansion of a network of cross-national organizations and associations. Just taking account of these changes in terms of everyday instruction in the classroom is enough to keep a conscientious teacher quite busy.

Life, however, is not so simple. Along with changes in the world in recent years have come changes in how we can look at or study the world. Current scholarship in international relations and in international education offers several images of the world around which to organize instruction. Each of these alternatives highlights certain aspects of the international environment and places less stress on others. As a consequence each holds somewhat different implications for the objectives, pedagogical techniques and curriculum materials to be used in an international education program. If social studies teachers are to continue to upgrade their instruction about the world, it is helpful to be familiar with these alternative views of the world and to be self-conscious about the world-view upon which their own instruction rests.

Becoming more self-conscious of one's own world-view or image of international politics is important because the objectives teachers set for themselves and their students, the instructional strategies they employ and the curriculum materials they choose are all conditioned by their images of the world. A teacher who views the world primarily in terms of nation-states pursuing foreign policies aimed at furthering their respective national self-interests will be likely to pursue objectives and adopt curriculum materials appropriate to this world-view. One such objective might be to help students develop an ability to critically analyze foreign policy decisions. The teacher might choose to use a game like the *Inter-Nation Simulation* or a book such as Abel's *The Cuban Missile Crisis* in pursuit of this objective. On the other hand, the objectives of a teacher who views the world in terms of a global society might be to help students develop a sensitivity to the political implications of mankind's increasing interdependence. In pursuit of this objective the teacher might use one of the new sets of curriculum materials focused upon the idea of "spaceship earth." Neither of these hypothetical teachers would be "right" or "wrong" in his or her approach for there is no single world-view which is *most* appropriate for international education.

As if this were not enough, there is another set of changes which the teacher must cope with. These are changes in youth and in the social scientific study of youth. The growing interrelatedness of the contemporary world is gradually altering the interrelationship of individuals with the international political system. In addition, this generation of children has lived almost entirely in wartime and has been the first generation to see televised international combat and diplomacy. The scope of politics for the young people of today is enlarging in the sense that their political "life-space" has broadened. Simply put, political issues now seem planetary in implication and a greater percentage of youngsters is aware of the issues facing humankind. Young people are living more intimately with the international system than ever before. It is now harder than ever to conceive of young people's "psycho-political milieu" as being bound by the nation-state.

Almost as if to mirror the emergence of a new kind of self-awareness and political consciousness in today's youth, political scientists have become increasingly interested in studying the political socialization of children and adolescents. Unfortunately, as we shall see, most research on children's political socialization has focused on their learning about domestic rather than global politics. Nevertheless, there is a small but growing amount of research on young people's international political learning. While this research is far from being "complete" and lags behind studies of children's domestic political learning, it already has a good deal to offer those interested in improving their international education programs.

In recent years, of course, a great deal has already occurred to upgrade the international education of children and young people. Schools have begun to place increased emphasis on non-western studies and on cross-national or cross-cultural comparative studies. Many educators are stressing the importance of increasing the intellectual honesty and objectivity of instruction about American diplomatic history and practice, other societies, and international affairs in general. New curriculum materials concerned with the study of the international polity and the international economy are being developed. Organizations such as the Center for War/Peace Studies, the Institute for World Order and the Center for Teaching International Relations, among others, have taken an increasingly active role in working with educators to improve the quality of international education. Teachers are evidencing a growing interest in international relations and foreign policy as textbooks, collections of readings, simulations and other educational materials become more available.

Our principal assumption in writing this book is that if international education is to continue to improve it is important that social studies educators become increasingly self-conscious about the images of the world which underlie their teaching—that is, their own world-view. In addition, it is important that they have an understanding of the process of children's learning about the world outside the United States. Neither being clear-headed about our own world-view nor understanding the world-view of young people, of course, is sufficient condition for continuing to improve international education but we feel they are very helpful conditions.

In Chapter 2 we review the current state of social science knowledge about pre-adult international political learning. In Chapter 3 we discuss alternative but not mutually exclusive ways of viewing the world about which we teach youngsters. These "world-views" have roots in classic and contemporary scholarship on international relations. Implicitly, they already form the basis of much that is going on in international education. Finally, in

Chapter 4 we consider the problems and issues involved in systematically designing world studies programs that try to take account of pre-adult international learning and alternative worldviews. The Appendix provides a bibliography on world studies and a set of "Guidelines for World Studies." These guidelines list potential objectives for world studies as well as include checklists to assist teachers in choosing materials appropriate for their students and community setting.

CHAPTER 2

Learning about the World

Every individual's particular configuration of political knowledge, beliefs, attitudes and values is developed over a lifetime through a process of political learning. Political learning begins in infancy, continues throughout life and is cumulative. Thus, political learning builds on itself to produce, at any point in time, the individual's particular set of ways of relating to politics. Through these the individual continues to engage in political learning and to further refine his or her political behavior.[1]

Political learning may occur formally—as when teachers lead their classes in the pledge of allegiance or a leading junior high school textbook asks students to "Write a short research paper on agreements with other nations that the Soviet Union has broken."[2] Or political learning may occur informally as when a teenager witnesses a street scene involving a policeman, or a child observes the teacher making an arbitrary decision about which members of the class are eligible for the next field trip.

In this chapter we will consider current social science research about children's and adolescents' international political learning, for the political learning of pre-adults in the contemporary world is not confined solely to learning about American national politics. The world into which children have been cast is one in which the political life of humankind is organized into many different types of political systems at different levels of social organization. Much like a cobweb these systems overlap and interpenetrate but are distinguishable. Just as in the Middle Ages when individuals were subjects of local fiefdoms, larger kingdoms and the Holy Roman Empire, so today individuals are simultaneously members of several overlapping and interpenetrating political systems. The typical American is thus a member of the international political system, the American national political system, and a variety of state and local level political systems.

Children are exposed to the notion that there are different and distinguishable levels of politics and government in a variety of ways. In the elementary grades the social studies curriculum is frequently compartmentalized into segments dealing with community helpers and neighborhood life, the political history of the United States, and world geography and history. At the high school level, courses on such topics as local or state politics, national government, and world affairs further elaborate the idea that individuals are members of several political systems. Outside of school, for both children and adults, the mass-media regularly "sort" the barrage of stimuli from the political environment into such categories as community affairs, local and state news, national news and world news. In a study of high school seniors, Jennings found that by the time they reach twelfth grade, American students are aware of and readily able to distinguish among these various levels of political life.[3]

As children develop they acquire political orientations toward the events, institutions and processes associated with each of the different political systems of which they are members. Thus, just as they learn about local, state and national politics, children also learn about international politics. They acquire political attitudes not only toward policemen, the Presidency and the Congress, but also toward the United Nations. Their knowledge of the political world includes not only knowledge about "how a bill became a law" but also about how nations negotiate with each other. Children's schema of political values includes not only preferences regarding civil rights but also preferences toward war, peace and imperialism.

The political knowledge, beliefs, attitudes, and values children develop toward global politics may be different from those they acquire toward sub-global politics. For example, research suggests that there may be a considerable difference in the attitudes children develop toward domestic and international political conflict. In a study of elementary school children, Hess and Torney discovered that by eighth grade children had not yet fully recognized the role of debate, disagreement and conflict in the operation of the national political system.[4] On the other hand, in a study of children aged nine to twelve, Targ found that by sixth grade children displayed a *realpolitik* international world-view wherein alliances and war were seen as important, legal, but aggressive mechanisms for promoting the "national interest" and the "balance of power."[5]

Differences such as these can apparently arise because the "object of learning," the international system, seems so different from the other political systems—national, state and local—which children are exposed to and about which they are learning. Former Secretary of State during the 1950s, John Foster Dulles, succinctly described a few of the ways in which the international system differs from sub-global political systems. Dulles listed six characteristics of national societies which he felt were largely absent in the international system. These are:

1. Laws, written or unwritten, which reflect the moral judgment of the community.
2. Political machinery to change these laws . . . as conditions change. . . .
3. An executive body to administer law.
4. Courts which settle disputes of a justiciable character in accordance with the law.
5. Superior public force which deters violence by its ability to apprehend and punish adequately any who breach or defy the law.
6. Well-being sufficient so that the people . . . are not driven by depression to follow ways of violence.[6]

Because of differences like these and others, the international system apparently offers youngsters contact points of political learning, and elicits roles and motivations which vary from those offered by politics at national, state and local levels. Consequently, the timing, sequence and content of youngsters' international political learning may differ from that of their political learning toward politics at other sub-global levels. The office of President, for example, stands as a highly visible, tangible representation of the authority structure of the American national political system. In their research with elementary school children, Easton and Dennis found that the Presidency offered children a personalized, salient contact point which facilitated their acquiring attitudes toward the national political system at a far earlier age than some theories of child-development might have predicted.[7] The international system, on the other hand, lacks one or a few strategic individuals like the President who stand as meaningful, palpable representations of the authority structure of international politics.

Similarly, except in times of international crises, domestic political events and issues are probably more likely to be seen by individuals as directly linked to their daily life-experiences than are issues and events in the international environment. Of course, in an increasingly interdependent world we can question how accurate this perception is. Nevertheless, questioning does not alter the fact that, for most people, most of the time, domestic political issues and events touch upon and activate a wider range of daily roles—such as student, housewife, mayor, doctor—than do international events. In this way, the international system offers opportunities for political learning which vary in intensity, type, duration and quality from those offered by political systems at the sub-global level.[8]

That children's international political learning may differ from their learning about politics at the sub-global level is an important point to keep in mind. For current research in political science on political learning has by and large not investigated children's learning about the world outside the United States. Hence, familiarity with this research is not sufficient for a better understanding of children's international learning. To gain greater insight into young people's international learning we must consider a much smaller group of rather disparate studies, most of which were not undertaken under the rubric of "political socialization." But before we turn to this research, let us briefly consider why there have not been more studies of children's international political learning.

Research on Political Learning

Since 1959 research into children's political learning has increased a great deal. While current research is not organized according to any single, overarching theoretical model, most political scientists have used the concept of *political socialization* to guide their inquiries into children's political learning. The notion of political socialization is derived primarily from the concept of socialization as used in anthropology, psychology and sociology.[9] In these fields the core meaning of socialization can best be described as that of induction, accommodation, inculcation—in short, that human learning directed toward the acquisition of the prevailing norms, values, roles, and cognitions of society. Socialization thus refers to a limiting and shaping process through which "individuals learn to become acceptable members of their society."[10]

Political socialization is the process by which an individual gradually learns the political knowledge, attitudes, values and behaviors accepted and practiced by the ongoing political system. Just as people are socialized toward patterns of beliefs and behaviors acceptable to our culture regarding sex, marriage, drugs, work and the like—they are socialized toward political life. The end to which political socialization functions "is the development of individuals who are integrated into the political realm of their culture; who accept the approved motives, habits and values relevant to the political system of their society; who transmit these political norms to future generations."[11]

Not all political learning, however, is political socialization. The concept of political socialization—like all concepts—has directed researchers' attention toward certain aspects of political learning and away from others. It has focused attention on that part of political learning related to the acquisition of the knowledge, attitudes, values and skills necessary for the persistence of the ongoing political system. In so doing, it has helped political scientists to better understand an important facet of the human condition; namely, the regularities of human politics through time and space. However, the concept of political socialization has directed researchers' attention away from investigating political learning which is unorthodox and does not conform to the prevailing political culture. As a result, the current body of research on political socialization is not very useful in helping us to understand how and why political systems change, and how and why some individuals do not acquire political orientations acceptable to the political system of their society.

Political socialization, then, refers to the induction of individuals into the prevailing political culture. As a result, it has naturally drawn attention to political learning about national political life and away from political learning relevant to the other levels of political life. Thus, the great bulk of political socialization research has investigated such topics as the development of children's knowledge and attitudes toward the Presidency and the Congress; the transmission of political party identification from parents to children; children's attitudes toward voting in national elections and their sense of trust and efficacy regarding national politics. Hence, in an era of expanding megatonnage and increasing globalization of the human condition, there has been relatively little research on children's and adolescents' international political learning. The tendency of the current research to concentrate upon one type of political learning (political socialization) at one level of political life (national politics) is understandable, yet regrettable. For our knowledge of the full richness and complexity of pre-adult political learning has suffered as a consequence.

Learning about the World during Childhood and Adolescence

When we think of the world as an object of political learning, it is natural to ask what aspects of the global system children learn about, what do they learn, and what are their primary sources of information and ideas about the international system. One can think about something as vast and complex as the international system in any number of ways. From the standpoint of the political life of the international system, perhaps the single most important type of actors in the modern world are the political communities we customarily call nation-states or countries. These are collections of people occupying a geographically bounded piece of the Earth's surface who are subject to a common set of political authorities. The surface of the planet is now a patchwork of well over one hundred such entities. We will begin by considering how and what young people learn about their own nation and other nations.

Development of a Sense of National Identity

How and when do children come to identify with their own nation? In 1951 the noted learning theorist Jean Piaget studied Swiss children's (ages 4 to 15) developing conceptions of their nation-state. He concluded that until they are five or six, children see themselves as the center of the social world and are relatively unaware of their broader environment.[12] Not until they reach ten or eleven do children conceive of their nation as a distinct entity and correctly perceive its relationship to their town and state.

Piaget also found that very young children display no consistent attachments beyond their immediate family. Increasingly with age, however, children begin to show preferences for their own nation and to see it as *terra patria*. This feeling is apparently based upon their ability to understand the relationship between their place of birth and residence, and their country. Finally, by ages 10 and 11 children had "more or less adjusted to certain collective ideals of the national community" and preferred their own nation to other countries. In essence, they had become Swiss.

Thus, learning to become Swiss or American or Russian, for that matter, may depend upon the development of children's general

Table I
The Development of Children's National Identity
From Jahoda Study

Age 6-7 (Grades 1-2)	Age 8-9 (Grades 3-4)	Age 10-11 (Grades 5-6)
Rudimentary concept of home country.	Concept of home country established.	Geographical and historical concepts in the stricter sense are beginning to be mastered.
Fails to understand "foreign."	Understands "foreign."	Political and economic ideas make their appearance.
Can name few, if any, other countries.	Can name other countries.	
No coherent space/time orientations.	Partial space/time orientation emerging.	

N for this study was 144 children interviewed for 45 minutes each. Data collected in 1962.

logical abilities. In a series of studies with Scottish children Jahoda amplified upon this idea by demonstrating that the development of national identity also corresponds to children's ability to make spatial and geographic distinctions.[13] And as Table I indicates this ability is apparently well developed in children by at least ten or eleven and in some cases even earlier.

In a study of 12,000 American elementary school children conducted in the early 1960s, Hess and Torney found children pass through three stages or phases on the road to developing a sense of national loyalty and identity.[14]

In the first stage, before grade two, children develop strong, positive attachments to their country and a sense of "we" for the United States and "they" for other countries. Their initial identification with the nation apparently has little cognitive content. Instead, symbols of the nation like the flag and the Statue of Liberty function as important objects through which "feelings of attachment can be socialized."

In the second stage children's concepts of their nation "acquire cognitive substance, including abstract qualities and ideological content." Positive feelings about the United States become focused upon qualities of the American political process such as "freedom" and "the right to vote" which "distinguish it most clearly from other countries." Table II (p. 12) illustrates how as children age, aspects of American ideology and the political process become focal points of their attachment to America.

Table II
"What Makes You Most Proud To Be an American?"
From Hess and Torney Study[15]

	Concrete/Material Aspects		Ideological Features	
Grade	Americans Are Generous	America Has Beautiful Parks	Americans Vote for Leaders	Americans Have Freedom
2	32%	37%	24%	52%
3	22	30	35	76
4	14	22	47	86
5	10	13	65	92
6	9	8	72	94
7	5	4	82	96
8	3	4	84	96

N's for each grade range from 1640 to 1786. Each student was to choose two aspects. Data collected in 1962.

In the final stage America "is seen as part of a larger, organized system of countries" and children develop a relatively mature perspective about other nations and relations with and among them. By this stage children have established a stable, highly positive attitude toward their nation which is basic to their future learning about politics.

Thus, while the process is complex and not yet fully understood, it is clear that the growth of children's attachment to their own nation starts early, proceeds rapidly (especially between the ages of six and ten) and culminates in the acquisition of highly positive national sentiments on the part of most children. In some ways this process may be analogous to the development of a sense of self. Developing a sense of self is predicated upon an awareness of others and their expectations towards one's behavior. Identification with one's own country ("we") may be predicated upon an awareness of other countries ("they") and the identification of peoples in those countries.[16] Strange as it sounds, stereotyping may also play a role in the process. Since young children lack the ability to logically organize their socio-political environment they use stereotypic thinking to first identify the salient characteristics of their own group and then, subsequently, to understand foreign peoples.[17]

Orientations toward Other Nations and Peoples

How do children and adolescents view other nations and peoples? As we will see momentarily, the answer to this question is "negatively" if the other nations and peoples are Communist or

Communist-affiliated. For the single most prominent conclusion to be drawn from the rather disparate set of available studies on the topic is that American children of the late 1950s and the 1960s were socialized into hostile and suspicious attitudes toward America's "cold war enemies." With a relaxation of tension between the United States and Russia and China currently underway we can hypothesize that the pattern of young Americans' attitudes toward these nations and their allies will change. Verification of the hypothesis will have to await further research but the reader need not wait for that. Rather, you can "test" this hypothesis by asking your own students the types of questions reported upon here and comparing your results with those described below.

Younger children's orientations toward other nations may not be as subject to the sort of ideological concern just discussed as those of older children. Jahoda found that while the 6- to 9-year-olds he studied were prone to judge countries similar to the home country favorably and to be "patronizing, if not hostile" to nations seen as strange, these judgments were not based on political/economic considerations. As Table III indicates, however, older children were more likely to justify their preferences on ideological grounds.[18]

Which national groups do children find especially attractive and desirable? In a study of children from eleven countries Lambert and Klineberg found that American children would most like to be British, Canadian or Italian if they were not American. As for the

Table III
Development of Children's Orientations Toward Other Nations
From Jahoda Study

	Ages 6-7 (Grades 1-2)	Ages 8-9 (Grades 3-4)	Ages 10-11 (Grades 5-6)
LIKES	Preferences governed by appeal of the unusual in the physical environment or by snatches of concrete detail fortuitously acquired.	More familiar countries liked and characterized in terms of trite clichés.	Preferences justified in terms of the positive characteristics of the inhabitants.
	Ages 6-7 (Grades 1-2)	Ages 8-9 (Grades 3-4)	Ages 10-11 (Grades 5-6)
DISLIKES	Presumed fleeting negative association established with names of particular places or countries; the sole exception concerns Germany, related to the war.	Either former enemy countries or "strange" places formerly attractive but now rejected because of misconceptions about their inhabitants; e.g., Africa, India.	Follow the lines of the contemporary East-West cleavage and are justified by conventional adult cold war arguments; e.g., Russia, China.

N for this study was 144 children interviewed for 45 minutes each. Data collected in 1962.

least desirable nationalities, the younger American children interviewed chose Chinese, Russian, German, Indian and Japanese with equal frequency. By age 14, however, Russia very clearly became the first choice with Africa a clear second as least liked. Lambert and Klineberg offer an interesting interpretation for their findings, stating that

> American children, who are taught to view their nation as first in peace and first in war capability, find it difficult to choose to be any other nationality, whereas choosing what not to be is far less difficult. The choice of Africans by a fairly large percentage of the children might be interpreted as some sort of generalization from prejudice toward the American Negro. Evaluative descriptions in this case stress the bad, aggressive, different, dominated, and uncultured features of undesirable peoples, with dominated becoming the major theme at age 14, paralleling growth in the political content of their responses ... American children appear to be concerned with political domination when choosing the Russian nationality as undesirable, and with cultural and environmental backwardness when choosing the African.[19]

In a study of fourth-, fifth- and sixth-grade Midwestern children, Targ discovered that as children grow older they increasingly see the United States as "strong," and Russia and China as "important."[20] Small changes were noted with respect to their beliefs about Canada. As Table IV shows, older children (grade six) also rated the United States more positively than did younger children. Conversely, they rated China and Russia more negatively. Again, ratings of Canada remained constant.

Targ argues that children's attitudes and beliefs toward Russia and China represent their socialization in an adult "cold war

Table IV
Children's Attitudes Toward Russia and China
From Targ Study

	Item	Age 9 (Grade 4)	Age 10 (Grade 5)	Age 11 (Grade 6)
"BELIEFS"	United States is strong	83%	87%	92%
	Soviet Union is important	58	69	81
	China is important	51	62	74
"EVALU-ATIONS"	United States is good	76%	90%	93%
	Canada is good	91	95	98
	Soviet Union is good	47	32	22
	China is good	49	22	16

N for study was 244. Data collected in 1967.

Table V
Children's Images of Russia
From Hess and Torney Pilot Study

Question	Grade	Yes	Don't Know	No
Russians are poorer than Americans.	4*	47%	14%	39%
	6	65	16	19
	8	66	18	16
In Russia people are forced to vote for whomever the Communists put up.	4	55	31	14
	6	85	11	4
	8	77	16	6
In Communism everybody works for the government, not for themselves.	4	31	36	32
	6	77	16	6
	8	74	18	8

*N's for each grade range from 98 to 195. Data collected in 1961.

dialogue, transmitted through home, school and media." On the other hand, their consistently positive orientations toward Canada probably reflect the fact that American children do not receive many negative messages regarding Canada from their environment. Hence, unlike their attitudes toward Russia and China, they maintain their initial positive evaluation of Canada.

As shown in Table V, Torney found the majority of children agreed "with the commonly presented image of Russia (lack of freedom particularly in voting choice, less wealth, and government control)." In addition, in the best tradition of "know thine enemy," the children had "quite accurate ideas about the relationship between communism and Russia" with 41% of the fourth graders and 91% of the eighth graders *disagreeing* with the statement that "All foreign countries are Communist." Further 44% of the fourth graders and 92% of the eighth graders *disagreed* with the statement that "All Communists are Russian."[21]

As for their attitudes toward Communism, the majority of children agreed with both the statement that the "Communists want to take over our country" and the even more loaded statement that "We can never relax as long as there are any Communists in our country." Most children at all grades (four to eight) also agreed that "It is not the Russian people who are our enemies; rather it is the men who rule Russia." This attitude may represent a way for children to displace aggressive feelings upon a small group while prescribing friendliness and tolerance for the majority of the people.[22]

A study conducted by Glenn in 1969 suggests that children's attitudes toward Communism had not changed as much as might have

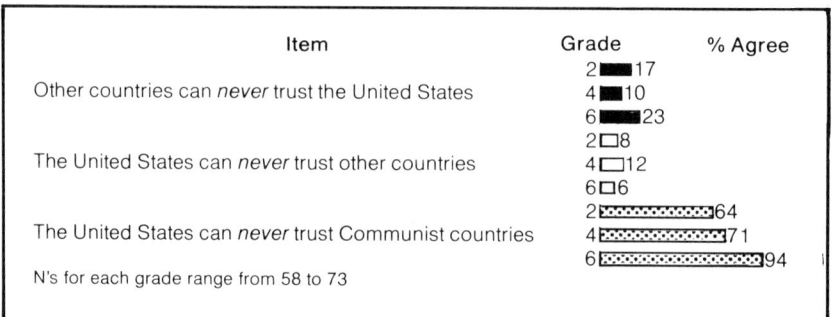

Figure 1
American Children's Trust in Other Countries
From Glenn Study

Item	Grade	% Agree
Other countries can *never* trust the United States	2 / 4 / 6	17 / 10 / 23
The United States can *never* trust other countries	2 / 4 / 6	8 / 12 / 6
The United States can *never* trust Communist countries	2 / 4 / 6	64 / 71 / 94

N's for each grade range from 58 to 73

been expected between the late 1950s and late 1960s (see Figure 1). Glenn concluded that

> ... most children felt the United States could trust other countries and, more than any other nation, the United States was worthy of being trusted. Most children also believed that communist countries could not be trusted. Suburban children felt more positive about trusting other countries than did rural and inner-city children [but] ... Differences between rural and inner-city children were slight.[23]

Glenn also found a sharp decline between second and sixth grade in the number of children who did not know what the word "Communist" meant. Sixty percent of the second graders indicated they did not know what the word meant whereas only 8% of the sixth graders indicated the same. He concluded that "the child's understanding of this particular word takes place sometime between the fourth and sixth grades and that this understanding encompasses highly negative feelings."

Older children and children from the suburban schools in the Glenn study tended to be more favorable in their feelings of acceptance of foreign children than were younger children, and children from the rural and inner-city schools. These findings are consistent with Jahoda's, who found lower-class children had more negative attitudes toward foreigners than middle and upper-class children. They are also consistent with those of Hess and Torney. Recall, they reported older children saw governmental leaders rather than the people of a particular nation as responsible for the way a country acted toward the United States. In making a distinction, then, between leaders of a nation and people in general children may displace their aggressive feelings on a small leadership group while still ascribing friendliness and tolerance to the majority of a nation's people.

Suspicion and anxiety toward Communist nations may not be confined only to American youngsters. In 1967 Morrison studied the attitudes of British secondary school students toward East-West relations and the "cold war."[24] His results were derived from the students' ratings of "My Country" (England), "China," "Russia," "U.S.A.," "Christianity" and "Communism." Both boys and girls rated their own country and the United States higher than Russia and China. Similarly, "Christianity" was rated much higher than "Communism."

Probing deeper into their concept of Communism, Morrison asked students to define Communism and tell why some people disliked it. Over 40% of the students couched their answers in ideological terms, characteristically describing Communism as atheistic and opposed to Christian teaching and churches. Twenty-five per cent defined Communism as an authoritarian form of government and another 25% employed broader socio-political concepts like classless society and social equality in their definitions.

A final source of data on children's and young people's perceptions of other nations comes from a study by Beyer and Hicks.[25] They sought to assess American seventh and twelfth graders' stereotypes and knowledge about major areas of the world, including Africa. Their data show young people associated images of disease and poverty with Asia and Africa. Russia, however, had the most clearly negative images associated with it and the students' images of Russia had a particularly political character not found with respect to other areas of the world (Table VI).

The students' knowledge about Africa was very limited. Students did most poorly on the questions relating to the history of Af-

Table VI
Students' Images of Russia
From Beyer and Hicks Study

Stimulus Term	Grade 7 (*12 years old*)	Grade 12 (*17 years old*)
Enemy	68.2%	75.6%
Dictatorship	46.4	70.0
Cold	46.3	81.6
Socialism	+	57.7
Violence	36.7	26.2
Powerful	28.5	+
Strange	25.8	+

+ = less than 25% of students associated term with Russia. N's are 845 for Grade 7 and 794 for Grade 12. Data collected in 1968.

rica before European penetration and best on the questions dealing with economic development, trade and products. Students from rural areas had lower scores than students from cities or suburbs. The study suggests that students may actually be learning misinformation about Africa rather than simply not learning any information at all. The source of students' misconceptions and lack of information about Africa, according to the authors, lies in the images of Africa presented by curriculum materials and the mass media.

Orientations toward the United Nations

Nation-states are not the only territorial groups into which we can think of humankind as being divided. Regional groups and organizations are of growing importance in the modern world. Perhaps the most well-known of these to Americans is the region comprising the European Common Market. For many purposes Black Africa also constitutes a territorial region as does Latin America.

Other important types of actors in the international system are large decision-making organizations. While national governments are probably the single most important decision-making units that make up the planet's organizational ecology, they by no means monopolize the scene. In the United States, for example, many state and local governments become active in foreign affairs by sending representatives abroad on foreign trade missions. In addition to national and sub-national governments there are an increasing number of international decision-making organizations and intergovernmental organizations.

Perhaps the most well-known non-governmental decision-making organizations that span national boundaries and have a substantial impact on our daily lives are international business firms. Such multinational enterprises as Olivetti, IBM, Royal Dutch/Shell and Nestlé are important actors in global politics. They have budgets which exceed the gross national product of all but a handful of the Earth's contemporary nation-states. In addition to multinational corporations, there are more than a thousand other international non-governmental organizations. Most of these organizations are composed of private or unofficial groups in different countries which have formed joint organizations to promote some common interest. They reflect religious, fraternal, scientific, business, artistic and humanitarian interests that cannot be bounded by the geography of the nation-state system.

Although there are fewer inter-governmental international organizations they are perhaps more familiar to most of us. The most conspicuous example of such organizations is the United Nations. In addition to the United Nations there are a number of other inter-governmental organizations such as the World Health Organization, the International Atomic Energy Agency, the International Labor Organization and the International Monetary Fund which have their own staff, budget and headquarters. The globe is encircled by an expanding grid of these organizations which cuts across the boundaries of nation-states and links national governments.

Unfortunately, research on young people's international orientations has chosen the nation-state almost without exception as the focal point of analysis. Thus, other important actions in the international system have not generally come within the purview of such analysis. Some research has been conducted on the United Nations, however, and it is to these data that we presently turn.

Children are aware of the United Nations and have some understanding of it as a political entity at an early age. Zurick, in a study of children 8 through 12 years of age from British Columbia, found that 58% of the 8-year-olds and 91% of the 9-year-olds in his sample had "heard of the United Nations."[26] The majority of the children saw the role of the United Nations as helping hungry children and making peace. Sex differences appeared in that twice as many boys as girls "perceived the United Nations politically, while more girls combine affective and objective descriptions of the United Nations into one."

Children's early awareness of the United Nations as a political organization is further evidenced by Targ's findings. Sixty-nine percent of the fourth graders in his sample and 65% and 76% of fifth and sixth graders respectively agreed that "the United Nations has most nations in the world as members." These children also saw a political role for the United Nations, with the great majority agreeing that the "United Nations discusses world problems." Per grade, 11% to 22% of the children were more aware of the functions of the United Nations ("discusses world problems") than were aware of its organizational membership and structure ("most nations ... as members").

Hess and Torney found that while children remembered discussing the United Nations "more than most other issues" on a list given to them, "they did not take sides in these discussions, probably because the United Nations is not presented as a controversial issue in the schools." They also found that while about 45% of the children believed the United States "ought to help the United Nations a lot more than we do now," only 35% thought the

Table VII
Attitudes Toward the United Nations as a Force for Peace in 1962 and 1969
From Hess and Torney and Remy Data

	Hess and Torney (1962)*			Remy (1969)+		
Grade	United Nations Keeps Peace	United States Keeps Peace	Don't Know	United Nations Keeps Peace	United States Keeps Peace	Don't Know
2	14.4%	70.7%	14.9%	—	—	—
3	27.3	62.3	10.3	—	—	—
4	48.9	40.2	10.9	33.7%	20.5%	45.8%
5	68.2	27.3	4.5	—	—	—
6	78.8	16.5	4.7	70.7	16.4	12.9
7	84.6	12.5	2.9	—	—	—
8	86.9	10.2	2.8	61.9	12.4	25.8
10	—	—	—	58.3	9.4	32.4
12	—	—	—	44.3	14.8	40.9

*N's are from 1630 to 1786 per grade, +N's are from 83 to 116 per grade.

United Nations should have more power than all its member countries.

What do children think of the United Nations as a force for peace in the world? In 1962 Hess and Torney asked children whether they thought the United Nations or the United States did more to keep peace in the world. Remy asked a smaller group of children the same question seven years later in 1969. Table VII suggests that young peoples' attitudes toward the United Nations may be changing.

The 1962 data show that as children grow older they increasingly see the United Nations as more important than the United States in keeping peace. Very few children responded that they did not know which did more to keep the peace. The data collected in 1969 present a different picture. From sixth grade on there is a steadily decreasing percentage of students who see the United Nations as doing more to keep the peace. On the other hand, there is a steadily increasing number of students who express uncertainty (through a "don't know" response) about the relative peacekeeping roles of the United Nations and United States.

Recalling the different dates at which these data were collected, we might speculate that the glamour of the United Nations has been somewhat tarnished by the growing sophistication of American youngsters and an increasingly apparent public image of the impotence of the United Nations as a force for world stability. In the early 1960s the charismatic Dag Hammarskjöld was Secretary General of the United Nations and the organization was under assault by Soviet leadership. The United Nations Organization was portrayed in the popular media as the center stage for the conflict between Communism and Democracy. There was considerable television coverage at that time of dramatic joustings between the shoe-banging Khrushchev and the reasoned responses of urbane Western diplomats such as Macmillan, Stevenson and Lodge. The Russians' vigorous "nyets" were consistently met by the positive presentations of security, disarmament and peace put forward by the Eisenhower and Kennedy delegates. However, with the increasing difficulties of the United States to muster a majority in the United Nations in the mid-1960s and downgrading of the glamorous aspects of the United Nations as a force for world peace—as witnessed by the shift in American personnel there from telegenic personalities to more prosaic politicians and diplomats—media coverage correspondingly declined as did the salience of the Organization in the public mind.

Additional information on attitudes toward the United Nations comes from the International Association for the Evaluation of Educational Attainment's 1971 survey of 3,000 American students ages 14 and 17. In this study Torney found that American students perceive the major activities of the United Nations relatively accurately. For example, 65% of the students knew that the United Nations' responsibilities included assistance to underdeveloped nations and keeping peace but did not include responsibility for custom duties, passports or the imposition of taxes in the United States. On the other hand, these survey data indicated the United Nations was not an institution about which students have extensive knowledge, a clearly developed image or strong positive feelings.[27]

A final source of data on the United Nations comes from the Purdue Opinion Panel surveys of high school students. The Measurement and Research Center at Purdue University has been conducting surveys of stratified national samples of high school students (grades ten, eleven, twelve) regularly since 1941. Several of their surveys have contained questions regarding the United Nations. The questions and the students' responses are presented in Table VIII (p. 22).

The students' answers reveal a moderate but consistent positive orientation toward the United Nations among American youth. This consistent, generally positive attitude toward the United Nations is probably reflective of the favorable attitude among the general adult population toward American participation in the organization. At no time since 1946 have more than one out of eight Americans thought the United States should withdraw from the United Nations. Since the mid 1950s the number has ranged be-

Table VIII
High School Students' Attitudes Toward the United Nations
Adapted from Purdue Opinion Panel Poll Data (© Purdue Research Foundation, 1949, 1951, 1963, 1966, 1971)

Poll/Year	Question
	(1) The U.N. should have the right to make decisions which would bind all members to a course of action.
	Agree / Disagree / Don't Know
22/1949	50% / 21% / 29%
	(78)* / (12) / (10)
69/1963	47 / 27 / 22
90/1971	(2) The United Nations should have the right to make decisions which would bind all members to a course of action.
	Definitely Agree / Undecided Probably Agree / Undecided Probably Disagree / Definitely Disagree
	32 / 27 / 20 / 17
30/1951	(3) Some important organizations in the U.S. have objected to flying the United Nations flag above the U.S. flag. Do you agree or disagree with them?
	Agree / Disagree / Don't Know
	28 / 55 / 17
90/1971	(4) The United Nations should be strengthened and given the power to control the armed forces of all nations, including those of the U.S.
	Definitely Agree / Undecided Probably Agree / Undecided Probably Disagree / Definitely Disagree
	22 / 18 / 22 / 34
90/1971	(5) The U.S. should be willing to give up some of its national power and independence to the United Nations in the interests of a better world.
	Definitely Agree / Undecided Probably Agree / Undecided Probably Disagree / Definitely Disagree
	19 / 25 / 25 / 29

*College graduates

tween only one out of sixteen and one out of twenty-one. Even during the Korean War when there was considerable public frustration with the lack of United Nations support for American actions in Korea, only 10% of the public considered the organization of "no use at all" and only 6% maintained that the United States should not "try to make the United Nations a success." Since then the figures on those two questions have ranged only from 3 to 7% and 2 to 4% respectively.[28]

For both United Nations questions (2) and (5) above, students reporting grades as "excellent" were more likely to approve of proposals to increase the decision-making powers of the United Nations than students reporting lower grades. Additionally, students whose future plans involved military training were more likely to favor restricting the authority of the United Nations (Questions 2 and 5) than students who planned to attend college.[29] These findings seem congruent with research on adults which finds isolationist attitudes more frequently expressed among the less educated than the more educated.[30]

Orientations toward the United States as an International Actor

In international affairs there are few well-developed moral and legal controls over what countries can and cannot do. Traditionally, nations have been seen as sovereign actors whose behavior is not limited by the same kind of restraints that are present in domestic situations. Given this backdrop, what role do children and young people see the United States playing in the international system?

Torney found a majority of fourth-, sixth- and eighth-grade children saw the United States as seeking to take a helpful and peaceful role in the world.[31] Over 60% of these children agreed that "America tries to prevent wars more than any other country." Similarly, high percentages responded yes to the question: "America helps people in other countries more than anybody else." Somewhat surprisingly, the majority of children also felt that the United States should take a friendly role toward the Soviet Union. Over 60% of them at each grade level agreed with the statement that "The United States ought to try to make friends with Red China and Russia."

Do young children see America as the world's leader? Torney finds that only 28% of the fourth graders, 27% of the sixth graders and 39% of the eighth graders queried agreed with the statement that "America is the leader of the world." Further, similarly low numbers of children felt that the United States was either the strongest country in the world or controlled the world. While 50% of the third graders in the sample agreed with the statement "It is all right for the government to lie to another country if the lie protects the American people," only 25% of the eighth graders did so. Thus, it appears that older children are more likely to apply stricter limits on state action than are younger children.

Targ found that "children increasingly saw the utility of United States interaction with other nations but were less supportive of policies that would relate to trust of other nations and disarmament." While the great majority felt the United States "should deal with other countries," they expressed a much less positive, internationalist orientation when asked whether the United States should trust other countries, agree with the Russians and Chinese to disarm and "do what most countries say we should in the United Nations."

Beyond these data there is little currently available information on younger children's orientations toward their nation as a participant in the international system. For young people of high school age there are some data available from the Purdue Opinion Poll which can help us gain a picture of adolescents' attitudes toward the international environment and America's role in it. Questions from the Purdue Polls are presented in Table IX.

When Communism is involved the students consistently see the role of the United States in the international system as an active one. Thus, the catalyst for favorable student attitudes toward American intervention appears to be engaged by Communist intrusion into the world environment. In 1966, for instance, the majority of students preferred military means to reorganize Vietnamese society to secure it from Communism rather than favoring a free election, referring the matter to the United Nations or withdrawing militarily (Questions 1 and 2). In 1971, at the height of public disenchantment with America's continuing involvement in Vietnam, 53% of the students were generally in agreement with the statement that "The U.S. should intervene when the Communists attempt to take over an Asian country" (Question 3). Communist presence in distant lands seems to override the generalized penchant for prudence expressed in Question (4) where 40% of the students definitely agree and 25% "probably agree" that the "United States should remain neutral in the event of violent political actions in newly emerging countries." Thus, the appearance of "Red China" in Question (5) appears to stimulate American students to take issue with the proposed diplomatic acknowledgement of the mainland Chinese. Only 15% definitely agree that the United States should recognize "Red China," and 30% definitely disagree. The negative images of and hostile attitudes toward Russia, Communism and the East found so consistently in the studies of elementary-age children reviewed earlier also seemed to be present here.

While perceptions of the right of the United States to intervene in the affairs of other nations seem Machiavellian, such attitudes may not be confined to American students. Morrison asked British secondary school students to choose which course of action the United States should take in each of the three following situations:

(1) The signing of a nuclear test ban treaty by the U.S.A. and Russia. The choice lay between strictly adhering to the treaty, or pretending to do so whilst attempting to carry on further secret testing.
(2) A civil war between communist and non-communist sides in a small but important country. The choice lay between intervention or non-intervention.
(3) A very serious quarrel between the U.S.A. and Russia. The choice lay between declaring war or not.

Table IX
Students' Attitudes Toward the United States as an International Actor
Adapted from Purdue Opinion Panel Poll Data
(©Purdue Research Foundation, 1949, 1951, 1963, 1966, 1971)

Poll/Year	Question	
77/1966	(1) If a peace conference in Viet Nam provided for free elections that could result in Communists being part of the Vietnamese government, would you favor such an arrangement or not?	
	Would	17%
	Uncertain; probably would	10
	Uncertain; probably would not	18
	Would not	56
77/1966	(2) If our opponents in Viet Nam refuse to negotiate, what should be the U.S. policy?	
	Withdraw all military forces	9%
	Continue to build up armed forces indefinitely	30
	Maintain our current strength as a holding force	34
	Refer the whole matter to the United Nations for decision	26
90/1971	(3) The U.S. should intervene when the Communists attempt to take over an Asian country.	
	Definitely agree	25%
	Undecided; probably agree	28
	Undecided; probably disagree	22
	Definitely disagree	21
90/1971	(4) The U.S. should remain neutral in the event of violent political actions in newly emerging countries.	
	Definitely agree	40%
	Undecided; probably agree	25
	Undecided; probably disagree	19
	Definitely disagree	14
90/1971	(5) The U.S. should give legal recognition to the government of Red China.	
	Definitely agree	15%
	Undecided; probably agree	21
	Undecided; probably disagree	29
	Definitely disagree	30
90/1971	(6) Over the next decade we must try to make the standard of living in the rest of the world rise more rapidly than in our own country.	
	Definitely agree	18%
	Undecided; probably agree	26
	Undecided; probably disagree	26
	Definitely disagree	28
90/1971	(7) Political and military affairs of European countries are no business of the U.S.	
	Definitely agree	19%
	Undecided; probably agree	16
	Undecided; probably disagree	25
	Definitely disagree	35

Approximately 75% of the students felt the United States should carry on further secret atomic tests on the rationale that Russia would do the same. In response to situation (2), two-thirds of the students favored American intervention in the civil war on the grounds that Communism must be contained. The one-third opposing American intervention did so on the pragmatic grounds that it would lead to an escalation of the conflict, a prophetic set of responses given the American experience in Vietnam. As one might expect, over 80% of the British students did not want the United States to declare war on Russia with the principal reasoning being fear of mutual destruction.

The Purdue Poll data in Table IX further indicate that neither the opportunity to "raise the standard of living of the rest of the world" (Question 6) nor the closer cultural and geographical ties of Europe (Question 7) elicits as interventionist a posture in students as did the questions about Communist threats to distant Asian lands. Thus, only 18% of the students agreed that the United States over the next decade should try to raise the living standard of the rest of the world (Question 6), a response congruent with some additional data to be presented momentarily. Only 19% definitely agree that the internal political and military structure of Europe is an important area of American involvement, that is, the "business" of the United States (Question 7).

Additional evidence on young people's perceptions of the proper role of the government in solving international social problems comes from data collected by Remy and Nathan from a national sample of high school seniors.[32] These data allow us to compare students' attitudes toward the government's role internationally with their attitudes toward the government's role at home.

As Table X shows, students favor an active role for the government in solving domestic social problems at the same time that they favor a less active and generous role for the state internationally. Thus, 90% agreed that the government "has a responsibility to try to reduce unemployment" and 89% agreed that the government "has a responsibility to try to do away with poverty in this country." While well over a majority of the students (66%) still gave an "active" response to Question (6), the number drops considerably when the mythological and symbolic issues of individualism and self-government explicitly enter the question. In their favorable attitude toward national government programs to accomplish social objectives, the students are reflective of preceding generations of Americans.[33]

As for role of the state internationally, considerably lower percentages of the students favor an active role. Only 54% agree that the "United States should give help to foreign countries even if they are not as much against Communism as we are." The loose Communist reference present in the question apparently does not

Table X
Student Attitudes Toward the Government as an Actor
Nationally and Internationally
From Remy and Nathan Data

International	% Giving Active Role Responses
(1) The United States should give help to foreign countries even if they are not as much against Communism as we are.	54
(2) We shouldn't think so much in international terms but should concentrate more on our own national problems and building up our strength and prosperity here at home.	30
(3) The United States should give economic help to the poorer countries of the world even if they can't pay for it.	52
National	
(4) The Federal Government has a responsibility to try to reduce unemployment.	90
(5) The Federal Government has a responsibility to try to do away with poverty in this country.	89
(6) Social problems here in this country could be solved more effectively if the government would only keep its hands off and let people in local communities handle their own problems in their own ways.	66

N's range from 1270 to 1345. Data collected in 1971.

evoke the national security bias discussed earlier. A similar percentage of the sample (52%) agreed that the government "should give economic help to the poorer countries of the world even if they can't pay for it." When the young people are forced to directly choose as in Question (2) between domestic and foreign expenditure, their enthusiasm for foreign aid is somewhat diminished and only 30% respond in "active" terms.

Upon reflection, it is not altogether surprising that young people should feel differently about the extent to which the government should take an active role in solving domestic and international social problems. A *Seventeen* magazine national poll of 2000 young people between the ages of fourteen and twenty-two also reflects the persistence of this domestic "activist" orientation.[34] Eighty percent of the *Seventeen* national sample expressed the opinion that the government was not spending "enough" for "helping the poor." Similarly, 66% felt the government was not spending "enough" for "medical research and/or care" and 69% felt "not enough" was being spent for "education." When the issue moved to the question of government spending for the "Indo-China war," "missile defense systems" and the "space program," only 4%, 9%

and 6% respectively thought the government was not spending enough.

Thus, it appears that it is much less complicated for young people to make the closure between self-interest and munificence in regard to domestic society than in regard to international society. When young people are forced to choose between family and friends and the safety of their nation, they choose, on the *Seventeen* poll, their family. Thus between the obvious well-being of their nation and the less-defined ingredients of interest and idealism that must be used to evaluate foreign aid, young people, not unnaturally, give domestic society their first priority.

Orientations toward War and Peace

In any society or social system, and certainly in one as vast and complex as the global system, there are a number of important social processes through which such values as health, money, natural resources and the like are allocated. In addition to the processes of foreign policy decision-making, these include internation conflict, collaboration, integration, trade, immigration, communication, transportation and cultural diffusion. While all these constitute important ways in which nations and other international actors interact with one another, studies of children have focused almost exclusively on their attitudes toward war and peace.[35] It is to these studies that we now turn.

How do children conceptualize war? Cooper found that coherent statements about war first appeared in English children around six or seven. By seven and eight children had "well-defined" ideas about what war is.[36] Younger children's images of war were concerned with the concrete aspects and objects of war such as guns, ships and airplanes. Older children's war imagery was focused on the consequences of war—fighting, killing and dying.

The fact that younger children think of war in terms of processes and older children in terms of consequences may be a result of societal expectations.[37] That is, younger children are not expected to be "too mature" and be concerned about the consequences of war but older children are.

In studying Swedish children, Rosell also found that as they grow older children define war in terms of the conflict underlying it. This ability to perceive the disagreements behind war is probably a function of cognitive development. That is, as children mature their capability in reciprocal reasoning—the ability to take or see the position of the other side—increases.

Children's imagery of war is much richer than their imagery of peace. The primary image of peace for younger children appears to be that of inactivity or tranquility corresponding to a state of mind or inner peace. Thus, Cooper, Alvik, Rosell and Haavelsrud in separate studies all found that younger children (12 years and under) see peace as simply the absence of war rather than as a social activity or process of international cooperation. Although these studies indicated some tendency for older children (ages 13-17) to see peace as a social process the prevalent image remained that of inactivity.

Why do children's and adolescents' images of peace lag behind their images of war—especially when developmental theory would seem to predict that as children grow older and become capable of reciprocal reasoning (about age 13) they should begin to see peace as a process instead of as the absence of activity? It may be that the concepts of war and peace as real entities are quite remote from children's general sphere of interest.[38] As a result children's growing structures of intelligence "have not yet applied to them" and adults do not provide explanations regarding "what lies at the bottom of conflict conditions on the personal as well as on the inter-group level." Thus, information about war is:

> continually present in the child's environment, through personal communications and mass media. Besides, most children engage in warlike play. All children also experience conflicts on the interpersonal and group levels. But peace is, both in personal communication and in mass media, to a greater extent conceived of as state of things which one enjoys, but which is not very amenable to active maintenance.
> "Peace" is commonly defined in such an empty way that the child sees no clear way of how to obtain it. Likewise, when peace is eventually obtained, the child considers it as a state of passivity more than as an ongoing process.[39]

Defense of country, friendship, honor, and the need to punish attack by another nation are principal reasons children give as justification of and causes for war. Children at all ages consistently express a willingness to go to war to defend their family, friends and country. This willingness to defend their major social groups may result from general socialization taking place before age eight in children, who learn to see such groups as important. Wars in defense of country are seen by children as just. As such they may well fit into an overall aggressive pattern of thought about international politics developed by children.

In his study of fourth through sixth graders Targ found children evidenced a general awareness of alliances, trade and peace treaties. Military alliances were seen to be "aggressive" and "important." Peace treaties were believed by approximately half of the sample to be "aggressive" and most children saw them as important. As for trade, fifth and sixth graders were more likely to see trade as "aggressive" than were fourth-grade students. Such findings suggest children develop an aggressive attitude toward international institutional arrangements at the same time that they learn to accept their importance.

In a major, recent* study of the attitudes of 2,667 American children in grades three through eight towards the Vietnam War, Tolley found that

> ...children regard war...as immoral, yet they express important qualifications to commitments based on principle. The majority acknowledges a duty to fight for national defense, and a smaller proportion justify conflict against communists...the children surveyed display no greater pacifism or anti-war sentiment than young people polled in the 1930's. The widespread opposition to the Vietnam war apparently has not generated revulsion for all war.[40]

Despite the evidence just reviewed, it is important to note that defense of family and country may not be a universally accepted rationale for war, even among older children. West Berlin public school students ages ten, twelve, fifteen and seventeen were asked to indicate whether or not a war should be started in response to a situation that threatened Berlin, their family, Germany, or an ally.[41] The consistent response at all age levels, for both sexes and across socio-economic levels was that a war should not be started. Differences in the cultural environment between English and Swedish children and the West German students might explain this finding. Thus, the special situation that Berlin and the people of Berlin have been in could have provided these children with experiences that resulted in a more peaceful attitude.[42]

It appears that children learn to see war as inevitable. Every study reviewed on the matter has found children feel war is necessary and likely. Cooper did find that the 8-year-olds rejected the necessity of war "on the grounds of the danger of physical hurt." The younger children, in effect, articulate a policy of deterrence derived from their own social order. They see war as unlikely

> provided that each party is well aware of his weakness or strength and whether he will win or lose, hence peaceful coexistence is in the

---

*Data were collected from January to early March, 1971.

nature of things. The child is clearly referring to his own social order. The order can be disturbed by "bullies," by ignorance of the order, and by a change in the order with age. The child appears to be implicitly familiar with rank-disequilibrium as a source of aggression.[43]

Fourteen- to sixteen-year-olds, however, appeared to make explicit assumptions about human nature, seeing "greed, lust, hate, desire for power" as instinctive human motivations "largely responsible for war" and increasing the necessity for war unless such feelings were held in check.[44] Haavelsrud's data support this finding. Ninety percent of his sample displayed "the belief that there is something inside people that causes war" and there was a significant trend for the German children to become more pessimistic about humankind's inherent nature as they grew older.

The American children surveyed by Tolley also felt it was extremely difficult to prevent war. Tolley explained:

> Those surveyed ... do not expect to inherit a peaceful world. ... An overwhelming majority of children, 91%, feel that stopping war is hard or very, very hard. ... Early in life, then, Americans learn to regard war as a regular feature of international relations.[45]

Why do children learn to see war as a necessary international social process? Tolley found both school and parent made important contributions to children's acceptance of war (Figure 2). As for schools, he explains that

> The greatest differences in our sample of children appear between boys attending Friends (Quaker) schools and military academy cadets. Our evidence confirms that formal instruction stressing a philosophy of non-violence or an appreciation of military values significantly affects children's outlook on war.[46]

Figure 2
Schools and War
From Tolley Data

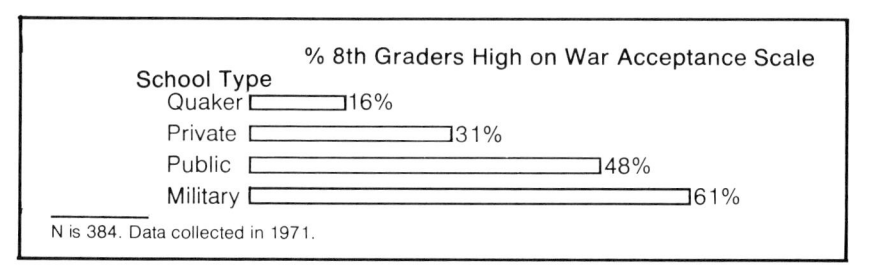

School Type	% 8th Graders High on War Acceptance Scale
Quaker	16%
Private	31%
Public	48%
Military	61%

N is 384. Data collected in 1971.

As for parents and teachers, Tolley concluded that:

> ... it is apparent that mother and father also influence general attitudes toward war. Patriotism may run in a family as much as religious conviction. Generally, children reflect the views of their elders. Comparison of children's responses with those of their teachers reveals that adults and children accept the necessity of war to about the same degree, and both groups appear equally certain that war will occur.[47]

In an era of expanding megatonnage and popular concern over the nuclear threat, research has not probed very deeply into children's orientations toward nuclear war. Escalona studied children between the ages of ten and seventeen from the New York area and found the danger of nuclear war was apparently very salient to these children.[48] She also found 39% of the lower-class groups mentioned the possibility of war whereas 62% of the lower-middle class and 77% and 100% of the middle- and upper-class children mentioned the topic. In addition, younger children, and those from lower socio-economic backgrounds, "seemed to regard peace as a matter of personal friendliness and intention," whereas the older, more sophisticated children "recognized the need for legal and military mechanisms to maintain peace."

In comparing responses of poor children with those of the middle-class children, Escalona concluded that

> many of the deprived children are so preoccupied by immediate pressing concerns, such as poverty, worry about school grades and jobs, and hostile elements in their immediate situations—such as gangs—that they have less "room" for the contemplation of more remote dangers.... However, once such children do recognize the danger to mankind's future existence they are more inclined to view it fatalistically and pessimistically. They express a wish for peace, but often no notions of how it might come about and relatively little expectation of a positive solution.[49]

In 1965 Allerhand reviewed the reports of several investigations concerned with children's reactions to societal situations with the potential for crisis.[50] Like Escalona, he found children to be aware of a nuclear war threat and disturbed by it. Allerhand proposed the following generalizations regarding children's reactions to international threat situations:

> ... feeling anxiety, children look for support and controls but find their parents inadequate because they, too, are experiencing the great rapidity of social and technological change. The confrontation with this emotional void pushes the children into a state of greater anxiety with lowered adaptive behavior and effectiveness in coping

with external circumstances. Some children, particularly those who are younger, academically unsuccessful or socio-economically starved, reveal a lowered awareness to factors beyond their daily living situation. Unable to turn to adults for stabilization, the children turn to anything available, usually an impersonal source such as television.[51]

To what extent do boys and girls differ in their orientations toward war? While none of the research has found extremely large differences between the sexes, the differences found have all been in the same direction. That is, girls are consistently more likely to look at war in terms of its consequences, to feel that war is not justified and to be less willing to go to war than boys. Boys, on the other hand, are consistently more willing to go to war, more opposed to Communism and not surprisingly show a greater interest in joining the armed services.[52]

Finally, Tolley's study provides evidence that the experience of the Vietnam war has affected the idealization of the President, widespread a decade ago. During the early 1960s several political socialization studies found that at a very young age children developed a highly positive set of attitudes toward the President, seeing him as a "benevolent leader" and a sort of kind, grandfatherly figure. This process was seen as an important mechanism through which children developed a long-lasting loyalty to the American political system. Tolley's data indicate that "the Vietnam war has significantly affected children's confidence in the chief executive" (Figure 3). Only 31% of the children Tolley surveyed in 1971, for instance, agreed that "President Nixon is doing the right thing in Vietnam."[53]

To this point we have focused on children's and adolescents' orientations toward war. We found that as they get older, children learn to see war as likely, necessary and, in essence, just. In an almost chilling way, young people apparently come to view interna-

Figure 3
"Does the President Always Tell the Truth about the Vietnam War?"
From Tolley Data

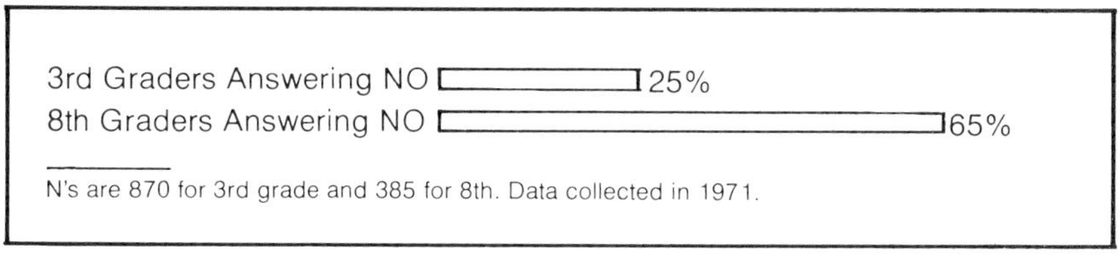

3rd Graders Answering NO ⬜⬜⬜⬜ 25%
8th Graders Answering NO ⬜⬜⬜⬜⬜⬜⬜⬜⬜ 65%

N's are 870 for 3rd grade and 385 for 8th. Data collected in 1971.

tion conflict as a regular, if troublesome, aspect of the international system. Boys are somewhat more favorably disposed toward war than girls. In addition, it appears the Vietnam war experience affected children's highly positive orientations toward the President.

Orientations toward the Future of International Society

In discussing children's orientations toward war we saw evidence that young people were not overly optimistic about the possibility of avoiding war in the future. How do young people feel about the future of the international system? Do they think the world they will inherit will be a better or worse place in which to live? The answer to such questions is of more than academic importance. For, as Chesterton said, our images of the future may be seen as "the prophetic past." That is, they represent the projection of our images of today's reality on tomorrow. As such, an understanding of young people's orientations toward the future can tell us something about their attitudes today, at the same time that it hints at what tomorrow will bring.

Remy and Nathan investigated young people's orientations toward the future of both international and national politics by presenting 1800 high school students with a set of predictions about 1990.[54] The predictions depicted hypothetical changes in American and international society relating to such problematic issues as the distribution of wealth, inter-group relations, the management of violence, environmental health, and the allocation of resources. Ten predictions depicting the status of these problems in the year 1990 for the national system and ten for the international were randomly presented in a single list. The series of predictions along with the instructions for responding to them and the students' responses for each statement are shown in Table XI.

The students' attitudes toward the future of national and international society were measured by calculating a national and international optimism/pessimism score for each student. Figure 4 (p. 36) illustrates the distribution of these scores. It clearly indicates that the students were considerably more pessimistic about the future of international society than they were about the future of national society.

Why were the young people surveyed less sanguine about the future of the international system? While we have no conclusive answer, it may be that differences in the nature or characteristics of the international system and the American national political sys-

Table XI
Students' Attitudes Toward the Future
From Remy and Nathan Study

Opinions about the Future

PREDICTIONS FOR THE 1990's. Suppose that someone predicts that the following changes will occur by 1990 (you will be about 37 years old then)—or before.

For each item, indicate in Column A whether or not you think it will or will not happen by checking one space. Guess if you are uncertain. *Then* go to Column B, *assume that the change will take place*, and indicate whether or not you approve of the change, (even if you don't really believe it will happen).

Column A
I believe it:

Column B
If it did happen, I:

will happen	won't happen	PREDICTIONS FOR 1990	approve	don't approve
49%	51%	All wages and prices will be controlled by the government.	35%	65%
21	79	The governments of all nations will agree to destroy all existing nuclear weapons and outlaw their use.	84	16
74	26	All information about a person—where he lives, works, his purchases and savings, his taxes, insurance, marital status, traffic tickets, etc., will be stored in a central government computer and be available to government officials and to organizations who wish to check credit.	28	72
17	83	Most countries in the world will be sufficiently secure militarily that military alliances will not be needed.	59	41
67	33	Less money will be spent by the federal government on defense and more on schools and health care.	89	11
46	54	There will be as many females as males in Congress, state legislatures, etc.	77	23
38	62	America's major urban areas will be vast slums.	7	93
73	27	There will be guaranteed income for all families sufficient to provide good food and housing.	77	23
65	35	Most of the oceans, lakes, and rivers of the world will be badly polluted.	6	94
75	25	Most big and medium size countries of the world will have their own atomic weapons.	10	90
33	67	Wars will be more common because most of today's problems will be more serious and still unsolved.	9	91
85	15	Blacks and Whites will be on much more friendly terms in the United States.	96	4
50	50	The United Nations will be more important and successful in settling disputes among nations of the world.	88	12
72	28	Russia and the United States will be on much more friendly terms.	92	8
53	47	There will be many violent protests and demonstrations in which many Americans are killed.	8	92
48	52	The rich countries will be richer and the poor countries will be poorer.	7	93
73	27	The bigger industrial countries of the world will economically dominate the smaller, poorer countries.	9	91
56	44	The smaller countries of the world will have joined together for their own economic and political safety and protection.	78	22
42	58	The rich in America will be richer and the poor poorer.	9	91
24	76	A few huge corporations like IBM and GM will control the economic and political life of the United States.	9	91

N's range from 1362 to 1451.

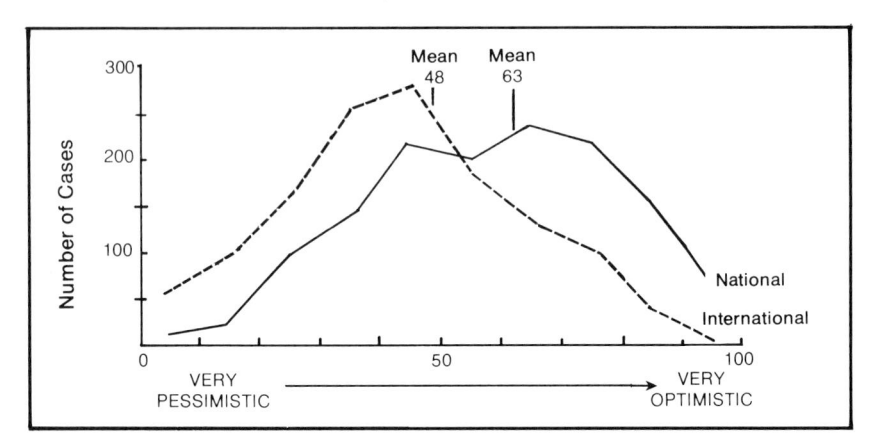

Figure 4
Distribution of Optimism/Pessimism Scores

tem affect the attitudes students develop toward the two systems. Recall that in the beginning of this chapter we pointed out that the international system can offer youngsters different contact points for political learning and can elicit roles and motivations which vary considerably from those offered by politics at national, state and local levels.

Thus, perhaps the more optimistic attitudes of young people towards their national political system find their roots in the very characteristics of the international and national systems themselves. International society is a system without centralized political authority. There is no single agent in the international system to manage change and control conflict. This is in fundamental contrast to domestic society. Perhaps most children look upon government as a kind of steering mechanism which manages the flow of history for the public good by promoting desirable changes and inhibiting undesirable ones. In the absence of centralized government in the international political system pre-adults might develop more pessimistic attitudes toward the future of international society than toward the future of national society. Without the presence of government to promote desirable changes within the international system they would see such changes as less probable. Also without the existence of a centralized system of authority to inhibit undesirable changes they would look upon such changes as more probable and consequently be more pessimistic about the future of international society.

Sources of Information about the International System

Where do children learn about the international system, its processes and actors? What are the sources of their attitudes, values and beliefs—the "agents" of international political learning? While there has been considerable research on the sources of young people's orientations toward the domestic political system—usually in terms of the relative potency of the school, family, mass media and peer groups as agents of socialization—there is less information available on the sources of children's international orientations.

What evidence we do have is remarkably consistent, however. Practically without exception studies have indicated that the mass media—especially television and newspapers—are the chief source of young people's ideas and information about the international system. Figure 5 below from Remy's study of high school students illustrates the pattern found in most studies with only minor exceptions.[55]

Figure 5
Student Perceptions of Their Primary Source
of Information and Ideas about Politics

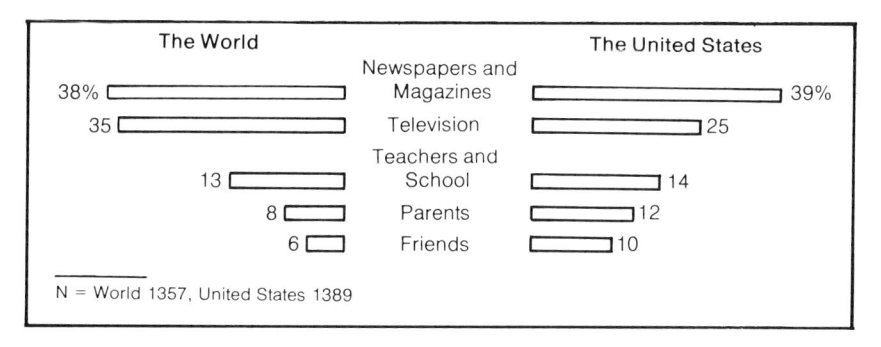

	The World		The United States
Newspapers and Magazines	38%		39%
Television	35		25
Teachers and School	13		14
Parents	8		12
Friends	6		10

N = World 1357, United States 1389

Lambert and Klineberg found that television, movies and to a lesser extent parents constitute major sources of information about foreign peoples for younger American children. As these children grew older, television and movies remained important and school sources such as courses and textbooks also became important. Parents, however, became "negligible" as sources of information. In their studies Alvik, Rosell, and Tolley all found the mass media to be the most important source of information about war for children. Tolley notes, for instance, that half of the children he questioned "said they watch news regularly, a larger proportion feel they learn 'a lot' about Vietnam from TV, and 80% indicate they have seen pictures of combat on news programs."[56]

In his study of the political learning of Australian children, R. W. Connell aptly describes television's role when he notes:

> Under the influence of the mass media, and particularly under the influence of television.... We can see that the global network of mass communications is indeed breaking down parochial tradition and bringing up the children as citizens of a global *polis*.
>
> It is a *polis*, though, which is only half-achieved.... And the involvement of the children in world politics is an involvement of emotional reaction, not an involvement of action or potential action. Only half of the classic exchange between the citizen and his city is present here. Television can show things to fear, things to be shocked by, things to amuse, things to like and things to hate, but it does not show the children things to do, forms of engagement. It simultaneously draws them in and holds them at a distance.... In the past it could plausibly be argued that political awareness expanded outwards, from local community to region to country and to international relationships. Children under the influence of television are introduced to the full range at once. Thus they come early to know about, and react emotionally to, those events which are most distant from them and least susceptible to influence exerted by the people around them. There is no chance for a sense of mastery or control to be developed in the smaller local context before the person comes into contact with events and issues more difficult to affect because at a greater remove.[57]

Although the evidence is limited on this important point, because television is rated by young people as an important source of information about international affairs it does *not* necessarily follow that it is also a major shaper of their international attitudes and values. The distinction is important and is suggested by Tolley's research. He found that in the case of the Vietnam war "children have learned basic attitudes about the conflict from mother and father at home."[58] In addition, as we saw earlier, Tolley found that schools play a role in shaping children's attitudes toward war. He concludes that while newspapers and television provide young people with information about war,

> ... parents and schools contribute jointly to a child's outlook on war, and their relative influence no doubt varies according to family, individual, and institution. On an issue as controversial as Vietnam, the relationship between attitudes of parent and child appears closer than the relationship between views of teacher and pupil, although for children whose parents rarely discuss the war, school exercises the greater influence.[59]

In this regard Torney has argued that at least part of the impact of the mass media upon students' attitudes was in the contradictions between what was seen there and what was presented in classrooms. She concluded that schools needed to deal more with the gap between the ideals of international cooperation and the realities of international conflict. In addition, they needed to make children generally more literate with respect to many different types of media.

To conclude, as might be expected there is no one source or agent of young people's international political learning. Various agents of political learning—school, parents, friends, the mass media and simply events themselves—interact in complex ways not yet fully understood. This said, it does seem reasonably clear that the mass media, especially in the form of television, do play an important role in children's international learning as do schools and parents. Beyond this, further research needs to be done before we can specify the sources of youngsters' international learning with any greater precision.

Conclusion

The reader should draw conclusions from this chapter with care, for most research has concentrated upon children's learning about domestic politics. Thus, contrary to any impression which might be given by this review, there really has been very little research on young people's international learning.

This means that it is risky to attempt to draw too detailed a set of conclusions about how, what, when and where children learn about international politics from the studies reviewed in this chapter. Instead, in conclusion our aim will be to abstract from the chapter several *ideas* which can help sensitize us to the international learning processes of our students. These ideas are as follows.

CHILDREN'S INTERNATIONAL LEARNING BEGINS EARLY IN LIFE

Children are born into a social world. In the course of their interaction with family, friends, the mass media and school they begin to develop orientations toward world politics. By the time they reach the intermediate grades they have developed a sense of national identity, a set of attitudes, beliefs and values about their own and other nations as international actors and about such international processes as war and peace.

Children's International Learning Is Cumulative

What children learn about the world at one age builds upon and is influenced by what they have previously learned. For example, what youngsters learn about war and peace at age fifteen is grounded in and shaped by what was learned at age twelve. In turn, learning at age twelve is conditioned by earlier learning. Through a continuing process of cumulative learning a political-self develops.

The Time of Middle Childhood (Grades Three through Eight) Is an Important Period in Children's International Learning

The period from about eight to thirteen years of age may well be unique in that it represents a time before too many stereotypically rigid perspectives dominate children's views of the world, and yet a time in which cognitive development is sufficiently advanced to make a diversity of viewpoints accessible.

The Beliefs, Attitudes, Values and Knowledge Individuals Develop about the World Differ

While this idea may seem obvious it is a useful one to keep in mind when planning instructional activities for children. Thus, not all of the children in the studies we reviewed thought war was inevitable, *some* thought it was preventable. Not all thought Russia could not be trusted, some felt the United States could trust Russia. The point is simply that while we have dealt in aggregate statistics in discussing youngsters' international learning, each individual student brings his or her own particular configuration of orientations toward the world. In some ways those orientations are very much like those of their classmates; in other ways they are totally unique to them.

The Mass Media, Especially Television and Newspapers, Play an Important Role in Children's International Learning

One of the most consistent findings of the studies reviewed here was the importance of the mass media as a source of children's ideas and information about the world. As children's window to the world, television has multiplied a thousandfold children's opportunities for incidental learning about various aspects of the international system.

Up to this point we have reviewed available research on children's international political learning. In the next chapter we turn to a consideration of alternative but not mutually exclusive ways of looking at the world about which we teach students. These alternative ways of looking at the international scene already inform much of what is going on in international education and have their roots in scholarship on international relations.

FOOTNOTES

[1] Norah Rosenau, "Political Learning in Children and Adults," (paper presented at the Third Annual Michigan State University Conference on Social Science and Social Education, East Lansing, Michigan, May 11–12, 1973), p. 5.

[2] Quoted in Byron G. Massialas, "We Are the Greatest!," in *Social Studies in the United States*, edited by C. Benjamin Cox and B. Massialas (New York: Harcourt, Brace and World, Inc., 1967), p. 183.

[3] M. Kent Jennings, "Pre-Adult Orientations to Multiple Systems of Government," *Midwest Journal of Political Science*, XI, No. 3 (August, 1967), 295–96.

[4] Robert Hess and Judith Torney, *The Development of Political Attitudes in Children* (New York: Doubleday & Company, Inc., Anchor Book edition, 1968), pp. 90–91.

[5] Harry Targ, "Children's Orientations to International Politics," *Journal of Peace Research*, II (1970), 79–98.

[6] John Foster Dulles, "The Institutionalizing of Peace," Address before the Fiftieth Annual Meeting of the American Society of International Law, April, 1956 (Washington, D.C., Department of State, Public Services Division, Series S—No. 46, 1956), p. 3 cited in Alger, "Comparison of Intranational and International Politics," p. 407.

[7] David Easton and Jack Dennis, *Children in the Political System* (New York: McGraw-Hill Book Company, 1969), pp. 198–200.

[8] James Rosenau, "Foreign Policy as an Issue Area," in J. Rosenau (ed.), *Domestic Sources of Foreign Policy* (New York: Free Press, 1967), pp. 11–51.

[9] The principal discussions using this typology of historical antecedents are found in Richard E. Dawson, "Political Socialization," in Richard E. Dawson and Kenneth Prewitt, *Political Socialization* (Boston: Little, Brown and Company, 1969) and David Easton and Jack Dennis, *Children in the Political System* (New York: McGraw-Hill, 1969).

[10] John J. Patrick, "Improving Political Learning in Secondary Schools," (paper presented at the 1972 Annual Meeting of the American Political Science Association, Washington, D.C. September 5–9), p. 2.

[11] *Ibid.*

[12] Jean Piaget and Anne-Marie Weil, "The Development Within Children of the Idea of Homeland and of Relations With Other Countries," *International Social Science Bulletin*, III (1951), 561–78.

[13] Gustav Jahoda, "Children's Concepts of Nationality: A Critical Study of Piaget's Stages," *Child Development*, XXXV (1964), 1081–92; "Development of Scottish Children's Ideas and Attitudes About Other Countries," *The Journal of Social Psychology*, LVIII (1962), 91–108; "The Development of Children's Ideas About Country and Nationality," *British Journal of Educational Psychology*, XXXIII (1963), Part I, 47–61 and Part II, 143–53.

[14] Hess and Torney, *Political Attitudes in Children*. Our discussion throughout will use results of the nationwide study and the pilot study. Some data from the pilot study have been presented by Torney in James Becker, *An Examination of Objectives, Needs and Priorities in International Education in U.S. Secondary and Elementary Schools*, Report to the U.S. Department of Health, Education and Welfare: Office of Education, Bureau of Research, July, 1969 (New York: Foreign Policy Association, 1969).

[15] *Ibid.*, p. 154 as modified from Hess and Torney, *Political Attitudes in Children*. Percentages do not always add up to 100 since children were instructed to choose two alternatives but some only chose one or "I don't know."

[16] Eugene A. Weinstein, "Development of the Concept of Flags and Sense of National Identity," *Child Development*, XXVIII (June, 1957), 173–74.

[17] Wallace E. Lambert and Otto Klineberg, *Children's Views of Foreign People* (New York: Irvington Publishers, 1967), pp. 223–24.

[18] Jahoda, "Development of Scottish Children's Ideas," p. 98.

[19] Lambert and Klineberg, *Children's Views*, p. 33.

[20] Targ, "Children's Orientations to International Politics," p. 90.

[21] Torney in Becker, *International Education*, p. 157.

[22] *Ibid.*, pp. 160-161.

[23] Allen D. Glenn, "Elementary School Children's Trust in Nations and Acceptance of Foreign Children" (paper presented at the Annual Meeting of the National Council for the Social Studies, New York, New York, November 24, 1970), p. 3.

[24] A. Morrison, "Attitudes of Children Towards International Affairs," *Journal of Educational Resources*, IX (1967), 197-202.

[25] B.K. Beyer and E.P. Hicks, "Images of Africa: A Report on What American Secondary Students Know and Believe about Africa South of the Sahara," Pittsburgh, Carnegie-Mellon University, 1968. (Mimeographed.)

[26] Elia Zurick, "The Child's Orientation to International Conflict and the United Nations: A Review of the Literature and an Analysis of a Canadian Sample." Paper presented at the International Peace Association, Third General Conference, 1969 (Assen Netherlands: Van Gorcum & Co., 1970), p. 187.

[27] Judith V. Torney, "The Implications of the I.E.A. Cross-National Civic Education Data for Understanding the International Socialization of American Adolescents." Paper prepared for presentation at the American Political Science Association, Chicago, Illinois, August, 1974.

[28] Alfred O. Hero, Jr., "Public Reactions to Federal Policy: Some Comparative Trends," (Mimeographed, undated), p. 13. A modified version of this paper appears minus specific figures on the United Nations in John P. Robinson, Jerrold G. Rusk, and Kendra B. Head, *Measures of Political Attitudes*, pp. 23-79. See also William A. Scott and Stephen B. Withey, "The United States and the UN, 1954-1966," *Journal of Conflict Resolution*, X (1966), 436-75.

[29] C. Van Horn and A. C. Erlick, "The American Way of Life: Politics, Patriotism, Isolation," *Report of Poll No. 90 of the Purdue Opinion Panel* (Purdue University: Measurement and Research Center, January, 1971), p. 7.

[30] Herbert McClosky, *Political Inquiry: The Nature and Uses of Survey Research* (New York: Macmillan Co., 1969), p. 81.

[31] Torney in Becker, *International Education*, p. 160.

[32] The data were collected by means of a paper and pencil questionnaire administered to high school seniors from all 50 states while they were attending a special educational program in Washington, D.C. in the winter of 1971. Forty-five percent of the students indicated their fathers were college graduates. Fifty-nine percent of the students came from homes where the father was employed in a professional or business executive occupation; 10% had "white-collar" fathers, 22% had "blue-collar" fathers and 6% had fathers in farm-related occupations.

[33] Alfred Hero, "Public Reaction to Government Policy," in Robinson, et al. (eds.), *Measures of Political Attitudes*, pp. 23-24.

[34] Editors of *Seventeen*, "You Tell What's Right and Wrong with America," February, 1971, pp. 116-27.

[35] For an exception see Ronald Inglehart, "An End to European Integration," *American Political Science Review*, LXI (1967), 91-106.

[36] Peter Cooper, "The Development of the Concept of War," *Journal of Peace Research*, II (1966), 1-17.

[37] Leif Rosell, "Children's Views of War and Peace," *Journal of Peace Research*, V (1968), 268-76.

[38] Trond Alvik, "The Development of Views on Conflict, War and Peace Among School Children: A Norwegian Case Study," *Journal of Peace Research*, V (1968), 171-95.

[39] *Ibid.*, p. 173.

[40] Howard Tolley, *Children and War: Political Socialization to International Conflict* (New York: Teachers College Press, 1973), pp. 36-7.

[41] Magnus Haavelsrud, "Views on War and Peace Among Students in West Berlin Public Schools," *Journal of Peace Research*, No. 2 (1970), 100-20.

[42] *Ibid.*, p. 117.

[43] Cooper, "Concept of War," p. 6.

[44] *Ibid.*, p. 7.

[45] Tolley, *Children and War*, p. 36.

[46]*Ibid.*, p. 125.
[47]*Ibid.*
[48]Sibylle K. Escalona, "Children's Responses to the Nuclear War Threat, *Children*, X (1963), 137-42.
[49]*Ibid.*, p. 139.
[50]M.E. Allerhand, "Children's Reactions to Societal Crisis: Cold War Crisis," *American Journal of Orthopsychiatry*, XXXV (1965), 124-30.
[51]Becker, *International Education*, p. 195.
[52]Cooper, "Concept of War," p. 7; Rosell, "Children's Views of War," p. 270; Tolley, *Children and War*, p. 40.
[53]Tolley, *Children and War*, p. 64.
[54]Richard C. Remy and James A. Nathan, "The Future of Political Systems: What Young People Think," *Futures*, (December, 1974).
[55]Richard C. Remy, "High School Seniors' Attitudes Toward Their Civics and Government Instruction," *Social Education*, (October, 1972), 594.
[56]Tolley, *Children and War*, p. 106.
[57]R.W. Connell, *The Child's Construction of Politics* (Carlton, Victoria, Australia: Melbourne University Press, 1971) pp. 128-29.
[58]Tolley, *Children and War*, p. 106.
[59]*Ibid.*, p. 120.

CHAPTER 3

Alternative Views of the World

International relations as a distinct mode of inquiry—separate from history, government, philosophy or law—has only achieved independent status and recognition in the last 30 or 40 years. Before this period, to be sure, there were historical narratives of wars or diplomatic machinations. There were also texts written about international law and philosophical treatments of how human beings and states should relate to one another. But only the press of the great conflicts of the twentieth century and the rapid ascent of universities to a prominent place in public life have combined to allow for the creation of a distinct field of study complete with a vast literature and separate "schools" of thought about international politics.

For all the complexity of the subject matter, three distinct frameworks for viewing the world may be identified in the study of international relations.[1] These frameworks have been widely adopted to explain global political activity. Each captures reality by filtering out some aspects of the total picture and highlighting others. The most familiar framework is to imagine international relations as if they consisted almost solely of the interaction of nation-states. An alternative framework is to look at the world as if it were a primitive society or "system" binding people in a web of global interdependence. Finally, there is a normative image of moral unity which is, it is frequently held, the underlying structure of our international political life.

Each of these conceptual frameworks emphasizes and illuminates some kinds of activity and passes over others. Each, then, is like the geographer's map which cannot be true to spatial relations, distance, and shape at the same time but can be fairly accurate to at least two of the three. Thus, each framework has distinct values and implications. Our purpose is to illustrate the limits, uses and assumptions inherent in each so that when they are employed in the classroom the teacher can be aware of each framework's implications. We began by examining a framework with a long tradition among scholars of international relations.

The State-Centric View of the World

The state-centric view looks at the world primarily in terms of sovereign nation-states pursuing their national interests through the conduct of foreign policy. The state-centric image of the world is the image of statesmen and diplomats, as well as many university scholars. In a sense, this framework for looking at the world is also an identifiable "culture" in which national policymakers have tended to operate. Foreign policy, so defined, is to protect against the dangerous and hostile forces at loose in a world where there are no international police and no courts with binding authority. To remain secure in such a world, nations must be prepared and willing to use force when necessary.

A perception of international society as an anarchic and dangerous domain of human activity is at the heart of the state-centric image of the world. According to this view, wars occur because there is little to stop them aside from self-restraint. Foreign policy is conducted in an arena of politics where there is no overriding compulsion except in the military capacity of each state involved in international politics. Since a condition of anarchy necessarily stimulates competition for military power, military power is sought for security. International politics is a domain of threat. Nations make alliances, conventions and treaties with the understanding that the ability to defend oneself is never given away. A state must always be sovereign or independent in order to secure and protect its customs, institutions, and inhabitants. Secretary of State Kissinger is a product of this culture. He recently stated, "No nation can make its survival dependent on the good will of another state if it has any choice about it."[2]

This view of international society as a state of anarchy and persistent emergency profoundly influences the conduct of foreign policy. It has buttressed presidential claims for enormous discretionary powers. It has prompted the Supreme Court in the 1936 Curtiss-Wright decision to hold that the warrant for presidential power in foreign policy is not in the Constitution but demanded by the necessities of being "equal and sovereign" which "is a condition of being a member of the family of nations."[3]

In addition, the state-centric view of international society as an arena of threat has made inevitable demands on national priorities. The Cold War allocation of over 30% of the national budget to foreign and national security policy, rather than to housing or community development or any other domestic need, is a fairly tangible indicator of the impact of the state-centric view on American society.

The condition of an international system characterized by the anarchic lack of a public monopoly of force is commonly viewed by statesmen and analysts as society at the edge of war. Force in this society is the common medium of exchange and power is the only means of gaining what a state needs. It is a domain of politics which recalls Cicero's lament, "What can be done against force without force?"[4]

The operant belief of American policy officials charged with foreign policy, like the view of statesmen of most other nations, is that foreign policy is "security policy." Other politics are concerned with justice or welfare. Foreign politics are concerned with survival and the uses of force. President Nixon confessed to presidential observer/journalist Theodore White during the 1972 campaign: "the American economy is strong ... it would take a genius to wreck it." But a presidential "mistake in foreign affairs would be fatal."[5]

The teacher who wishes to convey to students the images of the world prevalent among diplomats and strategists must necessarily focus on power, war, the national interest, the balance of power and the management of force. Indeed, much serious scholarship has been devoted to the instrumentation of power and its management.

The theme that the international system is dangerous and demands peculiar action not permissible in domestic society is also a common tenet of textbook wisdom. As one standard civics book, *Government by the People*, instructs its reader:

> The reason is clear. In a time of international tensions and crisis, democracies must act. Any device that will permit action without violating constitutional forms is indispensable. The methods we use

flout ideals of responsibility and popular control, but they seem to be part of the price we must pay for living in a disorderly world of sovereign nations.[6]

The intellectual foundations of the state-centric view, then, are found in the assessment of international politics as a *different kind of politics than domestic politics*. Unlike domestic politics, "realists" observe that international politics take place in an arena that has no central governing body. No superior international agency exists above each nation with either the authority or the power to make laws or settle disputes. The absence of such an agency above all nations means that a nation's compliance to international obligation is ultimately enforceable by individually concerned states. In international affairs, when all else fails, force is considered legitimate to arbitrate disputes. This is what is meant by saying that in the state-centric view, international affairs are anarchy which is a "state of war." Wars occur in international affairs because there is little to stop them. A former Assistant Secretary of State and Harvard economist, Thomas Schelling, has written that diplomacy, force and its resultant suffering are inseparable. For Schelling, to use force for no other end than the infliction of pain or suffering is "brute force." He writes:

> To inflict suffering gains nothing and serves nothing directly. It can only make people behave to avoid it.
>
> The only purpose, unless sport or revenge, must be to influence somebody's behavior to coerce his decisions or choice; to be coercive violence has to be anticipated. And it has to be avoidable by accommodation. The power to hurt is bargaining power. To exploit it is diplomacy—vicious diplomacy, but diplomacy.[7]

Alternatives to the State-Centric View

Stress on the use of force to gain policy ends is much less emphasized in the two other frameworks for viewing the world that we are about to examine. Alternatives to the state-centric view have arisen in modern international relations scholarship and in international education for many reasons. One of the principal reasons is that the nation-state itself no longer seems appropriate to the problems of the human race.

The nation-state, that geographic-political unit known by names such as France, Britain, the United States and China—whose people are bound together by common history, language and institutions—suddenly seems to be obsolete. After 400 years of being the irreducible, minimum fact of international politics, states are in a crisis whose contradictions defy simple explanation. On the one hand, states possess unparalleled sums of power. The ability to command and direct violence has become the most striking characteristic of nation-states. Yet military power does not seem to bring benefits commensurate with its cost. Force, for instance, is incapable of responding to world economic and social crises.

Moreover, a state's military power can no longer protect its citizens against enemies. Indeed, every American President since Harry Truman has warned the American people that the United States cannot survive an onslaught of nuclear weapons. The legitimacy and authority of the state were earned by a compact between the State and citizens. The State would be the citizen's fortress against capricious violence. The State would provide for the conditions of order and stability in which citizens could plan for their children or undertake their own livelihood. In this sense, the State used to be a precondition of society's benefits: health, wealth, justice and the like. In previous times a good life was impossible without a sound, viable State. In turn, the inhabitants of States "agreed," at least in theory, to be citizens, to pay allegiance, to pay taxes and to participate, if necessary, in the State's common defense. But if the State can no longer serve as the agent of its citizens' defense—in fact, if the State becomes the essential agent of society's ills—then the ancient agreement is shattered. And the "roof has been blown" off the historic shelter which nation-states once provided their citizens.

The monopolization of military force gave nation-states their definition. It also was an instrument of their will. The ability to direct violence against foreign states was a critical element of national greatness. Diplomacy and force were inextricably related. Yet the advent of irregular warfare (both urban and rural) and the expansion of force to the point where the use of force implies global suicide have largely paralyzed great military machines. Nuclear weapons have great destructive power. However, because the world is delicately balanced, the threat of force seems foolish if the "other side" can retaliate with assurance. States are unable to use nuclear attack weapons, and nuclear "blackmail" seems more and more unreasonable when the threat is disproportionate to almost any conceivable gain. Nuclear weapons have become impotent except in their symbolism of both national greatness and their grim reminder that all men are grouped together under the same dark shadow.

The nation-state is also caught in the profound surge of technological change which has brought most aspects of human interaction into closer proximity. There has been an internationalization of social and economic life. Where, for instance, insularity was once a self-conscious proud feature of Britain, now the scandals of Watergate cause as much controversy in England as the sounds of nearby civil war in Belfast. In America, our economics have suddenly become hypersensitive to world commodity markets. Economic sovereignty also has been breached in energy resources. America, for instance, increasingly relies on foreign resources for petroleum. In day-to-day economic life, our difficulties at the supermarket cannot be resolved by dealing with American farmers. Rather, the price of what we eat is influenced by an "international web of interdependence."

In this way foreign politics is no longer simply a matter of armed force meeting force. It is a close-knit interaction of economies, societies, organizations and statesmen. National policies, such as tax policy or tight budgets, can only be partly successful in controlling national economies. For the American economy, in an interdependent world, has become a captive to a gossamer "International Confidence," and the United States no longer is completely master of its economic destiny.

The Global System View of the World

One method of viewing the complexity of international affairs not encompassed in the state-centric framework is to see global politics as a vast system of social interaction analogous to any "primitive" social system without well-developed institutions, a central government or laws. Many who write about the international system use the phrase "spaceship earth" to depict this image of an increasingly interrelated complex world.

The "spaceship earth" view of the world is an essentially ecological image of international affairs. Ecology's "way of seeing" has shown us how the chain of life is interrelated and interdependent: neither the ocean, the air, the land nor the animal life which inhabit all of them can be "independent."[8] An ecological metaphor unites the seemingly distinct domains of biological activity—the ocean, the air, the soil and the life which inhabit them—into interrelated concepts. The global system metaphor highlights transnational behavior or that behavior which is beyond or breaks out of the definition and boundaries of "security policy" or "foreign policy."

What types of behavior and what kinds of international actors does this image refer to? Some of the chief actors are multinational corporations which have changed the character of international economic life so that it has become separated from national control. Today great corporations nominally based in Delaware, London or Zurich may have operations in one hundred countries. No one national headquarters will contain more than a fraction of their activities. Only a few such corporations, by shifting their reserves out of one currency and into another, can cause the value of national currencies to plummet or ascend. All of a nation's fiscal policies, balanced budgets, and tax policies can be invalidated by the power of major corporations which exist largely beyond the nation's control. By making "nonpolitical" investment decisions, international corporations can importantly affect national governments. The case of Chile in September 1973 provides a dramatic example. The world international banks and financial institutions took an increasingly dim view of Chilean President Allende's socialist-oriented domestic economic policy. Hence, they refused to extend credit to Chile. The result fueled ferocious inflation which contributed to the socialist regime's brutal removal by the Chilean military. Thus, multinational firms, which do not owe allegiance to any particular nation, can exert enormous pressure by their attitude toward Third World countries.

Similarly, the intellectual, cultural and scientific basis of national power is fast slipping from national control as technology, communication and multinational corporate resources expand. Where once a nation's greatness came from its ability to pour money into research, now research is international and capital is international. The dollar market in Europe has been more liquid than the market in New York for years; and computer and electronic technology is no longer found predominantly in America, but is diffused through the industrialized world. Not many years ago, the economic elements of greatness were concentrated and localized by the boundaries of the nation-states. Common stereotypes developed with some factual basis. Germans were hardworking and frugal. The British were great traders. Americans were inventive. Years ago, there was American physics or Italian design. But the compression of technological interactions has stripped these national labels of much of their significance. It is much more useful to speak of modern physics or contemporary design without national labels.

The global system view of the world, then, sees a number of factors leading to a growing interdependence or unity in the modern world. These are:

1. An expanding volume of worldwide trade and a dominance of the multinational corporation.

2. An expanding network of cross-national organizations and associations—fraternal, scientific and educational—that have developed a worldwide system of human interaction.
3. The inability to insulate domestic politics from foreign politics either within countries or between countries. Thus, the domestic politics of Arab nations or the Soviet Union can very much affect American relations with Russians.
4. The internationalization of social problems. The problems of survival, ecology, disease, scarce resources and the like are not manageable by nations. International cooperation is also necessary to combat the universal problems of urbanization, population control and crime.
5. An expanding homogeneity in humankind's culture and social institutions. Mass society, its artifacts, management and appeal now seem global in scope. International norms of individual conduct and State conduct are also becoming more uniform.
6. The appearance of alliances and economic unions which have formed the infrastructure for unifying wider portions of the globe. The European Economic Community now negotiates with the OPEC or Arab States as if each were sovereign. Moreover, the Common Market has been seen by many as the prototype for a politically united Europe. Many see the same pattern for the Soviet bloc and Latin America. The world's regional and transregional groupings are diminishing the role of individual nation-states in many of its historic functions.

Yet surely, one may say, security policy—wars and those who threaten them—dominates our attention and the attention of the media. If we concentrate on the global system do we not miss the critical questions of national life and death? Those who maintain that a global system perspective is useful would not deny the urgent questions of foreign policy—the politics of war and peace. But the ecological or systems view of the globe helps to move our attention to some of the interactions which are no longer contained or controlled by national policy. Of course, this view has limits. It is best used to illustrate economic, social and political "transnational behavior." Thus, the global system view helps us to visualize such forms of international interaction as the growth of regional organizations (the European Economic Community, NATO, the Warsaw Pact), the behavior of multinational corporations (ITT or Shell Oil), the relationships among international nongovernmental organizations (international labor unions and professional organizations), the globalization of questions of poverty (the Third World vs. the Industrialized World) and justice (what forms should an international law of the sea take?). The global system view does not help us understand the kind of politics Henry Kissinger engaged in when he suddenly went to Peking or when the Israelis moved against the Arabs in 1967. Or the kind of international politics President Nixon was referring to when he stated:

> We must remember that the only time in the history of the world that we have had any extended periods of peace is when there has been a balance of power. It is when one nation becomes infinitely more powerful in relation to its potential competitor that the danger of war arises. So I believe in a world in which the United States is powerful. I think it would be a safer world and a better world if we have a strong, healthy United States, Europe, Soviet Union, China and Japan, each balancing the other, an even balance.[9]

The politics of power, balance and strategy are much better illuminated by the classic state-centric world-view. But the cause and effects of urban disturbances from Lisbon to Tokyo and back through Columbia University, or the transfer of technology from America to Japan to Mexico are not highlighted by this vision of colliding nations which have no permanent friends or enemies, just interest. And the vision of an increasingly complex societal organization much like a national society, except on a global scale, does help capture some of the rapidly changing complexities of the last third of this century.

The Moral Unity of the Human Race: A View of the World

A third view of the world is found in the idea of world unity. This way of looking at the world sees international relations not in terms of the demands of statecraft or the imperatives of technology but rather in terms of *natural law*. It is the "idealistic" tradition of international affairs which is indebted to legal theory, theology and planners of a world state. The image is at least as old as the "Grand Unions" of nations proposed by Copernicus and Dante, and continues in the important work on world order and world federalism carried on by secular groups established in this century. The chief feature of this work is its rejection of power as a guiding principle to measure, understand or conduct international relations. Yet it is not mere Utopian musing. For the image of world community has motivated several American Presidents to pursue policy which is not now explicable in terms of "interest" or "security."

Thus, Woodrow Wilson brought America to war to establish a universal order in which liberal democracy could prosper under a

League of Nations. With the failure of the League, proponents of this vision called for "collective security." This represented an effort to manage the tendency of states to resort to force by depriving them of the legal right to use violence at their own discretion. This was the motivation and the rationale for the high hopes which accompanied the establishment of the United Nations. The purpose of the United Nations was to require nations to collaborate and repress the use of force as an instrument of national policy.

The illegitimacy of the classic balance of power with military force as the ultimate arbitrator of disputes was also the guiding vision of Dean Rusk. As Secretary of State Rusk exclaimed again and again, with real sincerity, the goal of American involvement in Vietnam was to see that acts of aggression and breaches of the "peace" were not tolerated by the international community. Alongside the legal sense of world community is the spiritual concept of world order which Pope John XXIII explored in his encyclical "Pacem in Terris." As H. J. Morgenthau, America's most prominent realist, concluded:

> To dismiss this as irrelevant . . . would be to fall into Stalin's error, when he had asked how many divisions the Pope has. The Pope indeed has no divisions, that is, no tangible power, but he has a moral authority that is susceptible of being translated into political attitudes, opinions and actions. The Pope, through his message to the United Nations, has used that moral authority on behalf of the peace, the United Nations, and its universality. Important consequences are bound to flow from that papal intervention. . . .[10]

Thus, all of global political activity is not explained by the state-centric or global system view of the world. As Professor Morgenthau recognized, the vision of what should be can be as powerful as armies and more lasting.

Implications of Alternative Views for International Education

Up to this point we have briefly examined three alternative visions of the world—the state-centric view, the global system view and the moral unity view. Each of these approaches to describing, analyzing and understanding world politics makes its own distinctions, has its own emphases and contributes its own circle of light. Each view of the world also holds distinct implications for international education and it is to these that we now turn.

The State-Centric View in the Classroom

The state-centric view of international politics has many policy implications for international education. For if political education is viewed as the preparation for survival, and if survival is contingent on preserving the State, then teaching allegiance to the State must be a necessary function performed by the State if it is to exist in a hostile world. In the state-centric view, therefore, teaching about other nations is important because they can be a potential threat or of possible value to one's own nation. International education guided by the state-centric view also seeks understanding of how States and people behave in order to harden the young to the necessities of a potentially explosive international situation. As one educator, R. C. Preston, explains:

> World understanding is not world agreement. Nor does it require that we condone despicable acts of individual foreigners or their governments. Sharp issues are bound to arise, and we are obliged to take a firm stand when they do ... we will be as hard as nails for the right and yet able to handle our adversaries with understanding, and we will have made a solid step forward toward national and international security.[11]

One of the major elements that pushed international education into the social studies was the emergence of the United States from World War II as the dominant global power. It was felt that an overhauling of international education was necessary. Children needed to be prepared for citizenship in a nation that had become a preëminent global power. They needed knowledge of peoples and places for whom they had an imperial responsibility. In addition, there was an urgent need to prepare children for responsible international activism lest the public mood revert to the isolationism of the inter-war period. Thus, the international education of the young was to both build a bulwark against a reversion of public attention to domestic politics and to service the demands of a worldwide responsibility. As the 1954 Yearbook of the National Council for the Social Studies put it:

> The United States in the second half of the twentieth century has drifted into world commitments which require global thinking by its citizens. At the same time these needs also demand highly trained personnel able to operate in other surroundings to carry out national aims and policies.[12]

Ignorance of the emerging Third World countries and the expansion of the Soviet challenge gave special urgency to federal encouragement of international education. A few months after Sputnik, Congress acted to counter the apparent Russian gains in education with the National Defense Education Act. The NDEA represented America's attempt to demonstrate to the Soviets and the rest of the world that Russian advances in rocketry were not reflective of any long-term Soviet advantages over the United States. Enormous funds were poured into a whole plethora of educational activities seemingly relevant to the Russian challenge. Engineering and science were given priority but there was also an enormous concentration of money put into area-studies. Indeed, the Cold War permeated the perception of the Office of Education's self-image at the time. The Office saw itself as a trainer of overseas specialists who would guard American interests against the Soviet menace.

This approach was to provide future leaders who knew enough about the world to apply that knowledge to the benefit of the national interest. Further, a realistic, state-centered approach to international education was not only necessary to train the young in the techniques of the pursuit of the national interest but also was necessary to avoid disillusionment when facing the brutal realities of international anarchy. As a 1958 social studies methods textbook states:

> A major objective in teaching international relations is to understand the basic conditions of inter-state relations. The cardinal fact of international relations is the existence of a multi-state system with emphasis on national sovereignty and personal loyalty to the national state. An attitude of realism toward international power politics is essential if American youth are to avoid disillusionment. The world has to be taken as it is. Talk of "One World," the brotherhood of man, and world government will not suffice to unite the dozens of sovereign states. In fact, in some parts of the world the multi-state system is growing stronger every day.[13]

There was also an assumption in the state-centric paradigm of international education that America would not prosper unless her example were relevant to the world. Somehow knowledge of the world was to be translatable into effective means of preserving our own institutions and making them acceptable to others. As the former director of the Office of Foreign Area Studies in the New York State Education Department, Ward Morehouse, has said:

> If our American ideals are to be preserved and to flourish in future decades, our youth must have knowledge of the world in which we live—particularly of the traditionally neglected but rapidly emerging

areas of Asia, Africa and Latin America, as well as the Soviet Union.
... increased understanding of other peoples and cultures gives us
sharper insight into our own institutions, problems and achievement
... also our national survival may well turn on the effectiveness of
this understanding.[14]

It is a bit embarrassing, in light of the more distasteful consequences of American power, to recall how such international education became a handmaiden of policy. Too often the state-centric viewpoint has been translated into a statement to the effect that support for United States foreign policy *must* start in the classroom. International education stemming from the notion of international anarchy often exceeded the bounds of being an exercise in policy conversion or even propaganda. Unfortunately it became, at times, an effort to foster an uncritical socialization into the fundamental norms of the public policy of an imperial power. As such, it was a practical step away from democracy.

Yet there is no reason to abandon the state-centric paradigm because of its past use, or misuse, in international education. For if one important purpose of international education is to help students gain an understanding of United States foreign policy, then to pass over the dominant and continuing conceptual world-views of policymakers would seem a mistake. Issues of foreign policy and international security, and questions of force, order and justice can usefully be studied by using the state-centered view. Questions regarding "the American posture toward the Soviet Union," or the "world-view" of a Henry Kissinger or Richard Nixon are difficult to meaningfully consider without a frame of reference that allows one to look at the world in terms of sovereign nation-states, each seeking its own interest and each concerned with its own position relative to others.

The Global System
and the Moral Unity of the Human Race in the Classroom

In this section, we will first sketch out what are the shared goals of international educators who subscribe to the image of moral unity or the world as a global system. These two approaches are not conceptually compatible with a traditional security focus. Rather, they search for means and mechanisms for the attainment of global peace. After reviewing the goals of these two domains of thought—which are usually fused or intertwined at the pre-collegiate level—we shall note some apparent limitations of both approaches.

The Moral Unity of the Human Race

From the "image" of the globe as a moral unity, educators have derived the notion of world citizenship. As early as 1928, W.G. Carr argued that unceasing interdependence of nations is both an indispensable process and an historical necessity. To Carr, we must oblige our youth to world citizenship because of the demands of commerce, religion, morality and security. Such a larger loyalty to the world community does not, in this formulation, contradict loyalty to one's own country any more than education of children to love their country stops them from remaining affectionate toward their families. Rather, the practice of citizenship in the world community is an act one takes merely by being aware of the events and conditions of world society, and valuing and empathizing with the lot of our fellow humans everywhere.

According to this view, then, the behavior prescribed for the world-minded citizen is "international understanding." This is the road to peaceful world order. International understanding apparently has three elements. First, there is the cognitive level of knowing about the diversity of humans in some detail. Second, there is a psychological predisposition which enables one to deal with foreigners in a friendly and sympathetic way. Third, there is a conscious effort to stimulate world-mindedness by extinguishing "negative nationalism." Nationalism and the nation-state are considered inappropriate for a peaceful, advanced, industrial world. At best they are suitable only as a way station on the road to world consciousness.

> We should re-examine the way and degree to which nationalism influences our teaching of social studies. Patriotism and loyalty to democratic values and institutions should continue as objectives but ways should be found by which these ends can be reached without... unthinking loyalty. Nationalism is a powerful force in today's world, a force very much needed in the creation of new nations. However, nationalism can be a negative force also, slowing the evolvement of those understandings across national and cultural boundaries so necessary to a cooperative and peaceful world.[15]

To international educators conscious of the moral unity of the human race, the traditional "civics" goals of educators—pride in national institutions and an understanding of the mechanics of these institutions—obscure the great technological and economic changes of our time. Thus, international education must concern itself with the replacement of the symbols of the State for the symbols of the human community. As Walter Laves wrote in the *National Elementary Principal*:

> Indeed, I believe that the real threat to the survival of free and democratic states lies in their reluctance to give up national symbols where they no longer are of utility or even threaten the attainment of agreed national, let alone international goals. ... Progress depends upon agreement among the nations involved. It depends also upon positive support within each nation at the governmental level and at the level of citizen understanding. At both levels, the key to progress is education.[16]

The Global System

For those who view the world as a global system, the fate of all of us is captive to ecological, security, economic, technological, and modernizing trends which hold us in a "spaceship earth." According to this view, the language of nationalism in education about international relations is inadequate to prepare us for the "historically new and emergent features of the human condition."[17]

Thus, unlike those who advocate education for international understanding, world citizenship or world-mindedness, those who see the world as an "emerging" social system or society feel that previous international education missed the "systemness" which is the essence of world change. Lee Anderson put the matter succinctly when he stated:

> Admittedly the picture of the world as a *planetary society* is not the best of all possible photographs of man's contemporary condition, and hopefully, it will not be long before our conceptual lenses become much more refined. But in the meantime this picture provides a comparatively better image of "the real world" than does our inherited image of the world as a mosaic of different lands and peoples or as a pool table on whose surface are arrayed self-contained balls called nation-states.[18]

The solution, however, to the education of youth into the emerging international system is frequently seen as the same by those advocating the global system view and those ascribing to the unity of man view. *It is to broaden the area of children's loyalty and concern.* Thus, educators who subscribe to the global system view hold that loyalty to the emerging global system comes about when people find the institutions of the existing State to be inadequate. But even then, their emotional commitment to the nation-state is so strong that only through a massive effort at propagandization can loyalties be shifted to a new global focus. As social-psychologist

Herbert Kelman once observed, since loyalties follow effective institutions, the building of global "functional interdependencies" (transnational organizations such as the Common Market, multinational corporations and the like) whose virtues can be communicated to the young will give substance to the fight against the barriers of the nation-state. The nongovernmental supranational institutions these educators presumably see as a "force for peace" are "actors" such as Gulf Oil, ITT and the International Union of Philatelists. Yet the evidence is contradictory and unclear about these new elements of international politics. Will, for instance, the role of large multinational corporations increasingly displace nations? Or will nations find a "handle" by treaty or state-practice to regulate great international firms? And will these firms, which tend to act to maximize profit, find their behavior congruent with social goals of the nations in which they do business? If not, then will the result be "peaceful" or will it exacerbate social tensions which can cause internal political upheavals which, in turn, can cause regional instability that invites military intervention by great powers?

Similarly, there is not firm evidence that international associations of scientists or increasing interactions of professions across the globe will greatly reduce conflict among nations. In 1914, a significant part of the German officer corps had studied in France and yet its nationalism was not quelled. Similarly, in 1914, the integration of the German and French economy was about the same as it was in 1967. Even in our day-to-day life, we know that seeing and having contact with people who are different really does not, by itself, contribute to understanding or a reduction of tension. In the long run, there are few facts to render an assured opinion that nongovernmental units are actually peaceful phenomena.

International educators of the global system persuasion, then, have set themselves a twofold task. One is to point to the possibilities for the development of new institutions in an embryonic international system. The second is to build a commitment among children to this nascent transnational system and its processes while its development is acknowledged to be just under way. International educators admit that there is more than a little manipulation needed to make this emerging world system psychologically viable for the young. Educators are concerned about "vestigial" attachments to the nation-state. But since the nation-state has a head start in commanding attachment and legitimacy, it is only natural that education is frequently seized upon as a "major force" which can break this vicious circle, where:

The failure to educate children for a global society strengthens the barriers against the development of such a society; the barriers against the development of a global society, in turn, help to account for the failure of the educational system to provide adequate preparation.[19]

Some of the normative and prescriptive implications which are inherent to the pedagogy of the world as a system are also common to the view of the world as a normative unity. Adherents of both visions of international society display a keen sense of mission—a kind of proselytizing imperative. Both indicate that if peace is to be firmly anchored in lasting institutions, there must be a correspondence in the way people feel about their fellow humans everywhere. Then viable transnational institutions and processes will, it is believed, take deep root and prosper.

There is also the feeling, common to both images and pedagogies, that the nation-state is doomed. Further, the process of the passing of nation-states could and should be encouraged by instruction of the young. Nationality should not be any more of a binding tie than one's commitment to the global commonweal. Developing loyalty in children can be achieved by instruction emphasizing global institutions and processes that fulfill people's social needs. As children come to view world community as the ultimate positive achievement they will develop new allegiances which extend beyond the nation-state.

This pedagogy of a new world order, especially as elaborated by social scientists who suggest the global-systems approach, deserves additional scrutiny. Take the matter of citizen participation in global society. At least the older, World Federalist vision very much implied citizenship and participation in the nation-state structures. But the new systems metaphor is an abstraction that yields very little immediate satisfaction about citizen participation. From the systems perspective citizenship is merely something akin to being a cell in a large organism. The cell has no means of controlling the organism nor any way of understanding how the various parts of the organism relate to each other. Even assuming that other parts of the world are undergoing the process of integration that Europe or the West has experienced, how does the metaphor of membership in global society aid individuals to "cope" or participate in their political destiny beyond mental acquiescence (if that is the meaning of "cope") or understanding (if that is the meaning of "cope") or toleration of their predicament (if that is the meaning of "cope")? It is not clear what an individual's obligations and rights would be as a member of the human species without some "narrow nationalist" base.

Does this imply that individuals cannot be taught to participate in the present international system? No, on the contrary, it is apparent that individuals can, do and should take part in consequential political activity not bound by the nation-state. Nevertheless, the means by which most individuals can ameliorate the more pressing problems of our age—poverty, ecology, and security—are still sub-global, and usually national and sub-national. Other means are just not apparent except to those technocratic elites of business, government or academe who subscribe to the global systems approach. And even these elites invariably have their behavior mediated by the State.

So then, if we are to teach young people how to "cope" with their global system's reality and to participate in the international community, it would seem only fair to see that they are familiar with the levers of potential change *within* the State that can affect behavior external to the State. Instruction in human destiny may save young people from "future shock." But if pedagogy is clouded by metaphors which deliberately pass over national institutions, as international educators sometimes suggest, in order to bring awareness to the larger human conditions, change in the larger system might be more obstructed than aided.

Thus, when considering the implications of the global-systems approach, one should remember that science and technology may well integrate the world—at least in a physical and economic sense—long before any viable international political structures appear. In the meantime technology tends to leave profound cultural dislocations. Moreover, whether or not we should welcome or encourage the most viable appurtenances of "modernization"— Holiday Inns, color T.V., Coca Cola—or should seek alternative strategies for the preservation of cultures under technological assault is one question which both scholars and educators might do well to address.

In addition, the abstract nature of a world-systems imagery may seem especially vacuous to the poor and the oppressed, and perhaps even to the middle-class. A system which is on as large a level of organization as the international system yields pedagogic prescriptions which would ring empty, one suspects, in Watts or Harlem. The international educator of the global system persuasion tends to put an emphasis on science. And science now has no cultural definition, for science is universal. The result of this approach is a search for social levels without local cultural substance or comfort. How meaningful would the following injunction, found in *Social Education*, about citizenship for a new age be to students in the inner-city?

> The importance of being aware of ... problems created by scientific breakthroughs can no longer be minimized by stating that "the chief duty of the American citizen is to vote." Vote he must for *national* survival—but for *human* survival, he must come to terms with science.[20]

The view that multi-level loyalties are desirable in an emerging transnational global society implies a kind of "assimilation." It suggests that one can instruct an awareness of what humans have in common rather than emphasize national or parochial uniqueness. Some international educators, therefore, would abolish "we" from the classroom.[21] Of course, if intellectuals think "we" is unnecessary it is one thing; but for others it is a living necessity. For those nations and peoples who are just regaining their sense of history, and for those whose identity is inextricable from their nation, propagation of multinational loyalties may only serve as a scholarly euphemism for national destruction.

International educators who hold the world-systems view feel that loyalties to the State and the international system need not be antithetical but rather can coexist side by side with each other. Moreover, international educators commonly suggest that we can hold meaningful loyalties to institutions at the nation-state level and to those that are emerging at the global-systems level at the same time. Yet this literature also asks for an abolition of ethnocentrism. What does this mean if it is not the squaring of the circle?

If our institutions were not felt to be superior, at least for us, they would be equal to all others. If they were equal to all others we should be indifferent to what institutions we do have since they would be no different than others. Thus, pride in our institutions is psychologically and logically useless if one accepts the initial assumption of the equality of institutions which international educators hold. For they cannot coexist on the basis of equality.

The international educator asks that we be ready to give up our national loyalty to the gossamer and still inchoate structures of the "emerging world system." But the problem of international education when it prophesies and promotes the world as a system is that individuals can too readily get trapped, in Matthew Arnold's words, "between two worlds, one dead [and] the other powerless to be born."

To the advocate of the global-systems view, international education for the future is critical. The idea is that we need a "pro" attitude toward change into the evolving world system, and that we must predict the future and shape it for the young. Granted, an ability to evaluate, react and even adapt to change is a necessary human skill which education should seek to foster. But should education always engender "positive" attitudes toward change? A question to be addressed might well be "How does one decide which changes to make and when and how can we deal with these programmatically rather than simply on the basis of good feelings or social engineering?"

International educators frequently predict that individuals will realize "self-conceptions of membership" in the developing world system.[22] They suggest that these "self-conceptions" be taught so as to make them "conscious" and "constructive." They feel that preparing the young for the future is a duty of those who have an understanding of current trends. Apparently, many international educators of the global-systems persuasion believe this insight can be transmitted with enthusiastic rational argument and instruction. Is it only self-assurance that prompts these educators to dismiss objections to global society as an "emotionally uncomfortable idea" because it only fills a need for some people's identity and cannot, therefore, be countered with rational argument? Or is it a kind of mandarin elitism that assumes some kinds of identity (even if they are "parochial") have to be subsidiary to the export of social science to the classroom? Perhaps the international educator sees the future and knows that if only he or she can win the hearts and minds of the young his or her vision will have substance.

Conclusion

The problem facing social studies educators today is not so much to choose one or another of the three frameworks just reviewed as "right" or necessarily better for all purposes. Rather, the problem is in insuring that we appreciate the implications and assumptions of each framework for international education, and that we are self-conscious about which world-view underlies these distinct frameworks. In essence, then, the task of the teacher is to locate suitable tools of explanation of an increasingly complex and fast-changing international political reality. Critical to this task is finding appropriate concepts which can convey meaning about international affairs which cover such seemingly diverse subjects as nuclear proliferation and Third World population pressures.

Concepts are, in fact, the key to finding the essence of the subject matter we wish to convey. In this sense, concepts stand in relation to reality as an artist's portrait does to a snapshot. The advantage and unique contribution of an artist is that he conveys a kind of highlighted essence which, shorn of the photograph's detail, conveys a reality which may not be evident in the thoroughness of the photograph. Concepts give organization to events, things and people who occupy seemingly diverse arenas of time and space. Take, for instance, the events in France in July 1789 and the events in Russia in October 1917 and in America in 1776. Without the concept of revolution it would be difficult to compare and contrast these phenomena. But with a unifying concept such as revolution we can begin systematic inquiry. We can ask, for instance, what are the causes of these kinds of phenomena; how do they differ and how are they alike?

Concepts embrace phenomena, help us order and classify them; concepts help us ask questions by which we can make comparisons within a class of phenomena and between different classes of phenomena. But the process of deriving conceptual frameworks and exploring their inner meaning has limitations. In physics, for instance, two different concepts "explain" electricity. For some purposes electricity is best conceived of as waves of energy. For other purposes electricity is usefully thought of as a stream of particles. In this way, concepts stand to reality like the plasticine overlays of a biology text with replicas of the cardiovascular system, the skeletal system, and the nervous system stand to the human body. Each sheet "explains" a good deal by ignoring a good deal more. Yet if we were to actually look at the total biological reality of humans at one time, the picture would be as crammed and detailed as a living person.

The three conceptual alternatives for viewing human social and international behavior are, then, like plasticine overlays. Each has a certain usefulness that highlights some kinds of processes, motives and events and obscures others. Each is akin, in this sense, to the relationship that a portrait bears to a snapshot. A portrait highlights what the artist considers the essential qualities of an individual—kindness, cruelty or mystery—while snapshots are detailed but flat representations that, by showing all, usually reveal little. The three concepts we offer here—the view of global moral unity, the view of a global social system, and the state-centric image of international politics—are not total explanations. As such *it is important that we not force students to choose among the three alternatives.* Rather, we should help them understand the limitations and use of each and form notions of "what is" and "what might be." The issue of central concern to us as teachers, then, should be: How can we help students become acquainted with, understand and use the wisdom of the scholars in their own lives?—Not: Which scholars will and/or should students choose as their heroes?

FOOTNOTES

[1] A more elaborate version of this argument first appeared in James A. Nathan, "The International Socialization of Children" (unpublished Ph.D. dissertation, Johns Hopkins University, SAIS, 1972) and James A. Nathan, "International Relations for Beginners: The World for Scholars and Children" (paper presented at the 1972 annual meeting of the American Political Science Association, Washington, D.C.). Since then the argument has become more familiar to international relations scholars. See Arend Lyphart, "The Structure of the Theoretical Revolution in International Relations," *International Studies Quarterly*, Vol. 18:1 (March, 1974), 41–75.

[2] *Washington Post*, February 5, 1973.

[3] *U.S. v. Curtiss-Wright Export Corporation*, 299 U.S. 304 (1936).

[4] Cited by Kenneth N. Waltz, *Man, the State and War: A Theoretical Analysis* (New York: Columbia University Press, 1959), p. 159.

[5] *New York Times*, October 10, 1973.

[6] James MacGregor Burns and Jack W. Peltason, *Government by the People* (Englewood Cliffs, N.J.: Prentice-Hall, 1969, 7th ed.), p. 500.

[7] Thomas C. Schelling, *Arms and Influence* (New Haven: Yale University Press, 1966), p. 2.

[8] Paul Shepard in Daniel McKinley et al., *The Subversive Science: Essays Towards an Ecology of Man* (Boston: Houghton Mifflin Co. 1969).

[9] *Time Magazine*, January 3, 1972.

[10] Hans J. Morgenthau, *Truth and Power* (New York: Praeger, 1970), p. 291.

[11] R. C. Preston, "World Understanding in the Curriculum," in *Teaching World Understanding* (Englewood Cliffs: Prentice-Hall, Inc., 1965), p. 108.

[12] W. G. Tyrrell, "Developing International Understanding in the First Two Years of College," in *Approaches to an Understanding of World Affairs* (Washington, D.C.: National Council for the Social Studies Yearbook, 1954), p. 383.

[13] J. R. Skretting and D. A. Arnold and Robert Weiss, "International Relations," in *Educating Citizens for Democracy* (New York: Oxford University Press, 1958), p. 323.

[14] Ward Morehouse, *The International Dimension of Education in New York State* (Albany: University of the State of New York, State Education Department, 1963), p. 1.

[15] William H. Griffin, "The International Component of Citizenship Education," *Social Education*, Vol. XXVII, No. 2, (February 1963), 73–74.

[16] Walter Laves, "The Changing Role of the Nation-State's Imperative Value to Things Beyond the Nation-State," *National Elementary Principal*, Vol. XL, No. 4, (January 1961), 35–38. Copyright 1961, National Association of Elementary School Principals. All Rights Reserved.

[17] Lee F. Anderson, "An Examination of the Structure and Objectives of International Education," *Social Education*, Vol. XXXIII, No. 7, (November 1968), 640.

[18] *Ibid.*, p. 645.

[19] Herbert C. Kelman, "Education for the Concept of Global Society," *Social Education*, Vol. XXXII, No. 7, (November 1968), 622.

[20] Daniel Roselle, "Citizenship Goals for a New Age," (Conclusions of the Civic Education Project Team), *Social Education*, (October 1966), 417.

[21] Chadwick Alger, "Some Problems in Improving International Education," *Social Education*, XXXII, No. 7, (November 1968), 657.

[22] Lee F. Anderson, "International Education: The Problem of Definition," in *An Examination of Objective Needs and Priorities in International Education in U.S. Secondary and Elementary Schools*, Report to the U.S. Department of Health, Education and Welfare, Office of Education, Bureau of Research, edited by James Becker, (New York: Foreign Policy Association, July 1969), p. 31.

CHAPTER 4

Designing World Studies Programs

In recent years much has been done to improve the international dimension of elementary and secondary education. Increased emphasis is being placed upon the study of the world outside the United States. Curriculum developers are evidencing more interest in cross-national and cross-cultural comparative studies of families, political and economic systems, religions, societies and cultures. Many educators are calling for increased objectivity and more intellectual honesty in the ways in which schools teach young people about this country, other nations, and international events and institutions. Historians and anthropologists are more frequently globalizing the study of world history and attempting to free historical accounts from the ethnocentric bias that characterizes many Western versions of humankind's heritage. There are more materials that expose students to non-American perceptions and interpretations of American life and of United States involvement in the world community. And the increasing variety of new textbooks, readings, films, simulations and case studies provides teachers with more choice and help in stimulating student interest.

These trends illustrate the considerable progress being made in improving international education in American schools. But education must be judged by the magnitude of society's needs as well as by evidence of past progress. Preparing young people to live constructively in the world of the twenty-first century means confronting the global issues of war, terrorism, pollution, shrinking resources, racial tensions, economic strife, and use of outer space. Viewed from this perspective, today's educational system provides little ground for complacency.

Improvements in international education, like improvements in education more generally, depend upon a great many factors: the insight and commitment of those making the changes; the clarity and appropriateness of the objectives and goals that guide efforts in this field; the extent and quality of the research and development work; and the degree to which the needed intellectual and material resources are identified and mobilized to assist schools and scholars in their efforts to improve international studies.

There are virtually endless opportunities to bring students into contact with the issues, enjoyments, concerns and problems of our increasingly interdependent world. But where should one begin among all the data books, bibliographies, film catalogues, listings of study/travel opportunities and computerized inventories of materials, resources and research findings? In the previous chapters we have provided some notion of alternative ways of viewing the world along with a review of current research, and knowledge about children's international learning. In this chapter we will suggest ways to provide students with the knowledge, skills, attitudes and values they need in an increasingly interdependent world.

Goals and Motivations

As we have seen, the beliefs, attitudes, values and knowledge youngsters hold about the world differ. These differences can largely be explained in terms of learned patterns of social behavior. The recognition that particular views of the world scene are developed from early childhood, are cumulative, and are produced by both formal (in school) and informal experience suggests that teachers need to be sensitive to the living/learning processes of students. When objectives or educational experiences are imposed upon students simply in order to satisfy a school policy or a course requirement, their impact is likely to be negligible.

Just as there are divergent views of the world, so there are differing opinions about the goals of international education. Nonetheless, there is considerable agreement among educators and lay persons alike that school curricula should help students develop the capacities to lead productive, meaningful lives. Guiding those who make decisions in this field are assumptions about the nature of the problems today's students will deal with as adults, the type of experiences most likely to enable them to develop the capacities to cope with these problems, and the most effective and appropriate ways to provide these experiences.

Our summary of research in Chapter 2 and review of alternative ways of viewing the world in Chapter 3 cannot and should not in and of themselves define the objectives of international education. They can focus attention on some of the issues which concern scholars and foster an understanding of the process through which students acquire their beliefs about the world beyond our borders. Hence they can help guide teachers in their efforts to facilitate young people's international education.

But what beliefs, what attitudes and what kind of knowledge best serve students? Our motivations and concerns as educators largely determine these choices. Teachers who see education, like military power, as a way of furthering national ambitions will develop programs quite unlike those designed by teachers who see education as a means of building better cross-cultural or global relations among people and nations. Those who view the heads of nations as the only major "actors" of the world scene will create programs with quite different emphasis from those who view students, scholars, civic and religious organizations, business interests and other institutions which operate across national boundaries as important "world actors."

Teachers, like editors, newscasters and historians, have the problem of deciding what to include—what to present to their listeners, readers, students. Different curricular content or emphasis produces different patterns of achievement. This is not surprising. If students are expected to learn certain content or skills, provision must be made for such learning in the classroom and in extracurricular activities.

The selection of content and curriculum can be thought of as a powerful tool for stimulating and directing the learning capacities of students, thus largely determining their achievement. If this be the case, the decisions and processes involved in selecting subject matter and experiences for inclusion or special emphasis are very important.

The development of units, courses or programs in world studies must, therefore, deal with such questions as: "What aspects of the world—that is what phenomena or objects—does one seek to help students understand?" and "What are the qualities, characteristics, or capacities one seeks to develop within students?"

A useful exercise for those who plan programs in this field might be to make a list of goals and purposes in international education or to consider some of the goals suggested by authors in the field. Such lists can be used to note preferences and priorities as well as to check the extent to which present programs are geared to those preferences. Smart suggests eight kinds of orientations for international education:[1]

(1) Introducing new ideas.
(2) Developing a synthesis of value systems related to an emerging world culture.
(3) Tracing national development.
(4) Studying and promoting national political power.
(5) Fostering mutual understanding and cooperation.
(6) Preparing students for life in a global context.
(7) Developing a creative attitude toward diversity.
(8) Furthering discovery of truth.

A simpler listing might include:

(1) Developing an appreciation of universal values.
(2) Contributing to national development and power.
(3) Building international understanding and cooperation.
(4) Working for world peace.
(5) Preparing for world citizenship.

Anderson suggests a threefold classification of educational goals: those oriented primarily "toward the well-being of the world as a whole," those oriented "toward the nation" and those oriented "toward being a citizen in a great democracy."

Yet another statement of goals may be found in the Appendix under the heading "Guidelines for World Studies." This list of objectives could be used to enable teachers to record their own preferences. The Guidelines also include checklists to assist teachers in choosing materials and experiences which seem appropriate for their students and community setting, and which are in keeping with the goals and objectives selected.

Checking Student Views

Just as knowing "where we are" is important in deciding what to teach, knowing "where students are" is generally accepted as a necessary and desirable basis for fashioning activities for the classroom.

As we saw in Chapter 2, there is a wide range of questions one can ask students to ascertain their orientations toward the world. Rather than try to list any specific set of such questions here, let us suggest different types of information about student orientations that could be helpful. It would be useful to have information about:

1. Students' images and perceptions of their own and other nations as actors in the international system.
2. Students' awareness and images of the functions performed by different international organizations.
3. Students' orientations toward international conflict and conflict resolution, particularly war.
4. Students' orientations toward international collaboration and cooperation, particularly peace.
5. Students' images and attitudes toward international power or influence.
6. Students' images of the problem of managing intergroup violence.
7. Students' images of and attitudes toward the problem of population growth.
8. Students' images of and attitudes toward the problem of global hunger and poverty.

Teacher Preferences

Ultimately, it is a combination of student orientation and teacher preferences that determines the selection of the resources, opportunities and experiences used to fashion a world studies program. But just as student attitudes reflect a composite of influences, so teacher preferences grow out of a variety of factors: awareness of accumulated experience in the field, differing views of the world, research findings, alternative strategies of instruction and theories of learning, as well as sensitivity to societal needs and problems and pressures from the community. The point here is that the program or curriculum in a school often reflects the assumptions, the preferences, priorities and understandings of those who make the decisions. Making these preferences known can help in the discussion of alternatives and in the process of reaching agreement and consensus; more importantly it can contribute to self-awareness, an important ingredient in situations involving human communication. Instead of smoothing over differences in outlook, educators ought to be open to each other's views and perspectives as they work to define the goals and purposes of international education. Developing or revising curricula should be an educational process in itself.

Educators and the World of Scholarship

Ideally, educators who design programs in the international field should be able to draw upon a vast body of international affairs scholarship. Too often, however, educators are stymied by a lack of knowledge about the nature and relevance of scholarship. What do scholars know or believe? How do they explain what is happening on the world scene? How can their explanations help teachers and students? Before trying to deal with these questions in a general sense, let us look at two developments which involve both scholars and classroom teachers—the media and intercultural training.

Media and International Studies

The mass media, especially television, have an immense influence on the peoples of industrialized countries and play an important role in youngsters' international learning. Through the media, young and old alike are constantly bombarded with facts, ideas, biases and impressions about what is happening in the world today. As we saw in Chapter 2, in our country many if not most young people look to the media as their major source of information and ideas about what is going on both nationally and internationally. Yet the media and the schools present information and interpretations of events in very different ways. The tensions between the government and the media, so obvious in the Indochina and Watergate convulsions, complicate the school's role of helping students learn to "read" the media. The schools thus have several complex tasks in relation to the media: to encourage intelligent use of media information, to counter possible misinterpretations arising out of media presentations and to place in perspective the varied and sometimes opposing postures taken by the media, the government and the schools.

Both sets of influences—schools and media—are mediated for the children by their tendency to extract latent messages and by their cognitive developmental level, which determines their readiness to understand material and the way in which they will resolve contradictions. Young people seek help in deciphering information and in understanding the discrepancies between school information and media information. Schools, for example, often tend to give the impression that by affirming our ideals or stance we have achieved them. Frequently, they give insufficient attention to the conflicts that exist. News programming in television, on the other hand, often seems preoccupied with shifting from one violent scene to another without continuity and with little effort being made to establish any relationship between the cause and effect.

The problem of violence and discontinuity in television news is especially acute with respect to the coverage of international events. Among the whole range of political phenomena in both systems portrayed by the media, national events are generally given greater priority than international events in terms of time and space. A typical national news presentation carries stories of everything from school board politics to the more spectacular features of our society. On the other hand, the small amount of time usually given over in the media to international events typically emphasizes the more calamitous aspects of international society. The quotient of misfortune and violence in international news coverage usually exceeds the quotient of misfortune and violence in national news coverage. International society, then, is all too frequently equated in the media as a society of hostility, explosion and catastrophe, while domestic society is characterized by a range of activities from harmony to disruption.

Whatever their shortcoming, however, the mass media have become so all-pervasive as to change dramatically the teacher's role from one of dispensing information to one of helping students gain a perspective on trends and events, only the surface of which is reported in the daily news. Preparing young people to appraise the information provided by the mass media involves giving them the ability to:

(1) Understand the use, limitations and liabilities of the whole range of media.

(2) "Read" public statements of governments, official denials, announcements from official sources and public relations messages.

(3) Detect typical biases in the media.

(4) Recognize the cultural contact which helps explain human behavior.

(5) Piece together fragmentary information from different sources in order to arrive at a plausible explanation of an international affairs issue or event.

(6) Perceive the process of news gathering and distribution, including the way in which certain biases are built into the process.

Given the importance attached to the media by youngsters, schools need to become more active participants in the process of media utilization. One way they can do this is by having students discuss in class what they have seen on television. A more fundamental approach would be to demonstrate how local, national and cultural biases influence the media's selection and use of information in such a way as to produce distorted images of other peoples and other nations. Educators need to design programs that will help students make the images in their heads bear a closer resemblance to reality. Basic to such programs are the goals of helping students see the world as others see it; creating an awareness of and adeptness in using alternative sources of information and evaluation; and developing a willingness to consider competing views of reality.

Understanding competing views of reality and seeing the world as others see it are emphasized in many intercultural education programs. Basic to such understanding is the culture concept. Scholars have many important insights to offer here. Before returning to the overall issue of scholarly input to designing international studies, let us look briefly at one approach to intercultural training.

Cross-cultural Training and Experience

Doing something that involves the actual crossing of cultural boundaries seems to be an effective way of learning about intercultural processes. As in the process of developing a sense of national identity, learning to relate to people in other cultures requires self-awareness, that is, a sense of one's own cultural identity. Ironically, until an individual has become involved with people from other cultures, it is difficult for him or her to experience his or her own culture. Persons who can consciously articulate their own self-images can begin to see how other people see them.

The culture concept—the notion that everyone has different ways of knowing about the world and of doing things—is a key idea in efforts to further cross-cultural understanding. The ways in which individuals interpret events, form judgments and reach decisions are largely culturally determined. We as individuals constantly send messages or present views to others, but if their cultural perspective is different from ours, they may misread our meaning and we may misinterpret their response. The capacity to understand the other person's response is crucial. Many intercultural problems arise from the failure of each party to recognize the assumptions and values held by the other.

One device for developing cultural self-awareness designed by the Human Resources Research Organization at George Washington University uses the concept of a "contrast-American." American assumptions and values in five categories—activity, social relationship, motivation, perception of the world, and perception of self and individual—are juxtaposed against a mirror image of these traits.

Competition, for example, is viewed as an acceptable motivating force in American culture and as unacceptable or demeaning in the contrast culture. The American sees the world as materials, to be exploited for human beings' benefit. The contrast-American sees the world as spiritual and human beings as inseparable from it. The American fragments personalities; in order to work with a person one does not need to accept the person as a whole. In the contrast culture one often cannot work with a person of a different religion, belief or code of ethics. The contrast culture does not portray a particular culture, but rather provides a contrast that helps make visible one's own culture. Such a scheme, especially when combined with role playing and simulations, can help increase understanding of American cultural traits as well as increase our level of cultural self-awareness.

* * * * *

The "information processing" approach associated with utilizing the media, and the "culture concept" basic to intercultural approaches are examples of contributions or insights by scholars which enhance the teaching of international studies. Many other contributions could be cited. Nevertheless, educators need to be aware that the scholar's mode of operation does not necessarily match that of the educator. International education tends to focus on the "here and now" world in which students must live, while scholarship proceeds in a conceptual time lag. The phenomena associated with nationalism, for example, appeared long before the term was coined or the concept became a useful tool for analysis. Similarly, the concepts and terms used to describe or analyze transnational phenomena today may suffer a lag. The remark has been made that "it is a poor historian who cannot predict the past." Scholarship, in other words, is most effective when dealing with past events; the "cutting edge" of scholarship may be no more significant than the speculations or queries scholars make about the future.

Just as scholarly conclusions are slow in emerging, so scholarship is notoriously slow in being transmitted to or accepted in schools. While there may be some merit in this deliberate pace, the fact that scholars are generally willing to share with teachers only the things they see as certainties may severely circumscribe their involvement in and contributions to school efforts. Yet it would be foolish for elementary and secondary educators to make decisions about international education without the benefits of the views of scholars—not just what scholars know "for sure," but what they believe are the crucial issues and developments that need attention.

The three current views of the world we summarized earlier reflect the state of international relations scholarship. Recall, they are:

(1) the world as nations
(2) the world as a system
(3) the world as a human community

We will first illustrate how scholars' view of international affairs might be applied to the day-to-day sort of things we are likely to discuss with students. Then, we will consider how their alternative views might be related to the overall design of curricula. As for the day-to-day types of questions each approach implies, consider the October 1973 War in the Mideast. The conflict and its aftermath were the kinds of events which could hardly escape notice. Using the "billiard ball" or the world-as-nations frame of reference, one might ask:

1. Who are the State actors involved in the conflict?
2. Who were their allies?
3. What was the "interest" of the states involved?
4. Were the interests of the superpowers the same (the Soviet Union and the United States)? Were they different? Was their behavior congruent with their interests?
5. What would "victory" look like for the combatants? Illustrate both sides' notion of victory. Is this the same as "success"?
6. What would be a "victory" for the superpowers (the Soviet Union and the United States)? What would be a livable settlement?
7. What "compromise" or settlement would be feasible for the combatants?
8. What are some of the reasons why agreement or settlement might be hard to achieve?

9. What are some of the means the States involved used to try to get their views accepted?
10. What are some of the factors that might make a settlement more likely now than in the past?

The world-as-systems approach, on the other hand, emphasizes essentially non-military issues. Thus, questions appropriate to the Mideast or other circumstances might be:

1. Who were the non-State, international actors involved (oil companies, OPEC, the Palestine Liberation Front, the United Nations)?
2. What were their interests?
3. How did they behave? Was their behavior congruent with their interests?
4. What non-military effect did this conflict have on other regions? (The Common Market, Latin America, individual countries, for instance, suffered from an oil embargo.)
5. What non-military reaction did these areas and countries exhibit? (I.e., Japan changed its diplomatic posture toward the Arabs and broke with the United States in the face of a potentially crippled economy.)
6. What effect did domestic opinion in the various regions of the world have on the conflict? Before the conflict, during it and afterwards? Was domestic opinion important? How?
7. Did any new, non-military, international relationships result from the conflict? Where? Describe.

Finally, moral issues are critical to all judgments of international affairs. However, they involve a different kind of analysis with different criteria or epistemologies. We know something is "right" in different fashion than we "know" how much oil the United States lost because of the embargo. Questions appropriate to the world as a human community view might include:

1. Who were the actors (State and non-State) and what were their moral positions?
2. Which actors seemed to be more morally justified in their goals?
3. Were their policies morally congruent and proportionate to their ends? Did their ends justify their means?
4. How did the moral issues differ from the legal issues of the actors involved?
5. Were any new moral or legal principles developed or established as a result of this conflict? What precedence do these principles have historically (e.g., the right of displaced peoples to homelands or the uses of international police forces)?

6. Is there a difference between the party's moral position and international standards?
7. Are the ethical positions of these parties valid? What are your criteria (e.g., the greatest good to the greatest number, the oldest international law, etc.)?
8. Can there be a difference between justice for a group in a specific situation and the "needs of the international community"?

As can be seen from the above examples, each of these frameworks emphasizes some aspects of the global activity of man and leaves out others. The state-centered framework is probably the most familiar of the three, largely because educational systems are operated and perpetuated by governments. Given the traditional and continuing emphasis on national history as the heart of civic or social education, the "world-as-nations" outlook still tends to predominate in the schools. Now, however, there seems to be more scope for competing viewpoints. The "world as human community," which has long had the visionary support of various philosophers, educators and lay persons alike, can now find a place in the educational system. The notion of "world as system" is also beginning to enjoy more prominence, due in large measure to the new perspectives afforded by space exploration and the obvious effects of global economic interdependence.

For purposes of deciding what kind of program best serves the students in a particular school, these frameworks can be used as the basis of a series of overlays, through which the relevant factors listed so far—student orientations, teacher goals and preferences and available resources and opportunities—can be matched up with each other and with the most appropriate conceptual approach. The overlays should reveal the degree to which all the variables or ingredients overlap or coincide, as well as the extent to which they fall into one or more of the scholarly frameworks summarized in Chapter 3.

Designing lessons or curricula utilizing the data and process outlined here might proceed like this:

(1) Students are asked to draw pictures, write or record a statement of what they believe the world will be like in 1990. A second exercise might be to ask them to indicate what they believe they will be doing at that time.

Teachers might be asked to do the same exercise. The questionnaire discussed in Chapter 2 could be used for this purpose.

(2) Checklists and questionnaires are used to elicit student beliefs and knowledge about other peoples and cultures and issues such as poverty, war, energy, pollution.

(3) A list of generalizations supported or suggested by research is made available.
(4) Statements representing alternative views of the world are presented.
(5) Information about available opportunities, resources and expertise is made available.

The exercise involves individual students, then groups, and ultimately the entire class in a process of sifting and sorting through impressions, preferences and other data, and developing a stance that takes into account as many of the elements and as much of the data as are consistent with the position taken by all: individuals, groups and the class as a whole. The teacher's preferences regarding goals and objectives would, of course, come into play through the selection of materials prior to the exercise as well as in the organization of the class, but much of the activity would be structured on the basis of student input.

A less free-wheeling approach would be for the teacher, after collecting data about student interests, attitudes and knowledge of world affairs, to develop a series of activities, lessons or situations in which students would not only learn about but reveal their preferences regarding the alternative frameworks posed in this volume.

Students could be assigned readings and reports, followed by class discussions of the merits or usefulness of the alternative frameworks in their effort to better understand world affairs.

For viewing the world as nations, for example, students might read from publications such as:

> *The Anatomy of Foreign Policy Decisions*, Dean Rusk, Department of State, Washington, D.C., 1965.
>
> *Armed Intervention: Under What Circumstances?* Education Development Center/Social Studies Program, 15 Mifflin Place, Cambridge, Massachusetts, 1970.
>
> *USA Foreign Policy*, Kirsten E.A. Borg (ed.), McDougal, Littell and Co., Evanston, Illinois, 1974.
>
> *Issues Today.* A series produced by the Department of State, Washington, D.C.

Simulation games, such as the following, might be used:

> *Internation Simulation*, Science Research Associates, Chicago, Illinois.
>
> *Dangerous Parallel*, Scott, Foresman and Co., Chicago, Illinois.

If the world is being viewed as a system, the class might read from materials such as:

> *Intercom #73*, "Teaching Toward Global Perspectives," Center for War/Peace Studies, 218 East 18th Street, New York, New York.
>
> *Organizations Among Nations*, American Education Publications, Education Center, Columbus, Ohio 43216.
>
> "Beyond the Nation State," Lester Pearson, *Saturday Review*, February 15, 1969.
>
> *World Society*, John Burton, Cambridge University Press, New York, 1972.

The world as a community stance would have students read from materials such as:

> *The Learning Society*, Robert Hutchins, New American Library, New York, 1969.
>
> "The End of American Independence," Lester Brown, *Saturday Review/World*, December 18, 1973.
>
> "The Humanist Manifesto," *The Humanist Magazine*, September/October, 1973.
>
> "The Ideal of Human Unity," Irv Aurobindo, *UNESCO Courier*, October, 1972.
>
> "Education for Mankind," John Goodlad, *International Understanding at School*, UNESCO Curricula No. 26, November 1973.

A variety of visual materials, new texts and supplementary materials, together with the mass media, are beginning to communicate a more accurate sense of human similarities and differences.[2] Problems which transcend national boundaries are also receiving more attention in both formal and non-formal educational settings. New maps of the planet are being developed which show shared ethnic and cultural interests, ecological perspectives, overlapping social and economic concerns, as well as geopolitical configurations.

The massive amounts of data available in world studies have such a scope and variety that any one best curriculum selection seems highly dubious. Learning to sift and sort through this mass of data in order to separate the significant from the trivial is crucial. Utilizing the insights of scholars and the benefits of related research can improve the process, but perhaps even more important is increased interaction and greater self-awareness among student, parent, teacher, and scholar alike.

In a world where defensiveness coexists with integration, hostility with cooperation, and nationalism with transnationalism, nations compete with each other for scarce resources, but at the same time find it in their own self-interest to cooperate with each other and integrate their behavior with other nations. The Soviet Union and China purchase wheat from the West despite a long and bitter history of mutual distrust and ideological contention. And all the rhetoric about national interests and sovereignty has not prevented governments from making literally thousands of functional agreements designed to provide needed services across national boundaries. It should be a major aim of international education to provide a context that can encompass isolation and integration, diversity and unity, aggression and cooperation.

International education today requires knowing facts, how to use them and how to find or create new facts, "the art of the utilization of knowledge" as Whitehead defined education. If international education is to be improved, educators will have to bare their efforts upon what is known both about the world and how children learn about the world. We hope this book provides helpful information in these areas.

FOOTNOTES

[1] Reginald Smart, "The Goals and Definitions of International Education: Agenda for Discussion," *International Studies Quarterly*, Vol. 15, No. 4, (December, 1971), 442–464. By permission of the publisher, Sage Publications, Inc.

[2] See especially *Man: A Course of Study* (Cambridge, Massachusetts: Education Development Center, Inc., 1970).

Appendix

PART I
A World Studies Bibliography

PART II
Guidelines for World Studies

PART I
A World Studies Bibliography

A. Background Reading and Sources of Materials for Teachers

Books

Becker, James M., and Howard D. Mehlinger, eds. *International Dimensions in the Social Studies*, 38th Yearbook. National Council for the Social Studies, Washington, D.C., 1968. Offers a setting and a framework for international studies. Emphasizes the need for new perspectives in many related areas.

Becker, James. *Education for a Global Society*. Phi Delta Kappa Educational Foundation, Bloomington, Indiana, 1973. Outlines some of the imperatives of globalism, provides a perspective on transnational participation, and offers some guidelines for global education in schools.

Bobrow, Davis B. *International Relations—New Approaches*. Free Press, New York, 1972. Provides an overview of new approaches and suggests a basis for evaluating both new and more traditional approaches. Lists sources of change and provides examples of newer methods of analysis.

Brown, Lester. *In the Human Interest, A Strategy to Stabilize World Population*. W. W. Norton & Company, Inc., New York, 1974. An interdisciplinary analysis calling for immediate efforts to stabilize the world's population and abandon the pursuit of super-affluence.

Burton, John. *World Society*. Cambridge University Press, New York, 1972. An analytical interdisciplinary approach which views world society as a total environment. Describes ethnic, political, economic and ideological systems and discusses decision-making, roles, non-national activity, problems of perception, values and conflict. A clear demonstration of a systems approach.

Castel, Helene. *World Development*. Macmillan, New York, 1971. A book of readings that raises questions about basic goals and values of development; attempts to place the development process in a context of human dignity and justice.

Commoner, Barry. *The Closing Circle; Nature, Man and Technology*. Alfred Knopf, New York, 1971. A lucid description of ecology, and suggestions for some needed changes in economic thinking if we want to survive.

Falk, Richard. *This Endangered Planet*. Random House, New York, 1971. Argues that preoccupation with the warfare-threat system has kept us from dealing with poverty, racism, overpopulation, and diseases; calls for massive redirection of human energy and material resources.

Fisher, Roger, ed. *International Conflict for Beginners*. Harper & Row, New York, 1969. A handbook on the analysis of recent international affairs; uses current problems in presenting ideas; a pragmatic non-moralistic approach emphasizing "Yesable Propositions."

Gordenker, Leon. *The United Nations in International Politics*. Princeton University Press, 1971. A number of experts provide answers to such questions as: "How can we understand the United Nations?" "How can we assess the prospects for the future of the UN?"

Hoffman, Arthur, ed. *International Communication and the New Diplomacy*. Indiana University Press, 1968. Specialists in various fields discuss what their respective disciplines can bring to the study of interpersonal and intergroup relations across national boundaries, and what the diplomat can learn from their findings.

Lovell, John P. *Foreign Policy in Perspective.* Holt, Rinehart and Winston, New York, 1970. An introduction to some of the complexities of the foreign policy process in the United States. Provides a useful guide for making independent assessment of foreign policy.

Meadows, Dennis. *The Limits of Growth.* A Universe book, New York, 1972. Predicts a world-wide collapse within a century unless the growth of population and industry is halted and a "global equilibrium" established.

Reischauer, Edwin O. *Toward the 21st Century: Education for a Changing World.* Alfred A. Knopf, New York, 1973. Argues that the universal problems faced by humankind require international negotiation which in time requires an informed citizenry educated in a new and radically different way. Better understanding of the outside world and changes in attitudes toward other people are seen as crucial to human survival.

Russett, Bruce M. *What Price Vigilance? The Burdens of National Defense.* Yale University Press, 1970. A dispassionate, objective analysis of why expenditures for national defense are so high and what some of the consequences are for American politics, the economy, and the society.

Sprout, Harold, and Margaret Sprout. *Toward a Politics of the Planet Earth.* Van Nostrand-Reinhold, New York, 1971. Explores the possible revolutionary effects of the threat of world-wide ecological catastrophe on the organization and governance of our world. Shows how the dilemma of rising demands and insufficient resources is producing important changes in the power and policies of nations.

Ward, Barbara and René Dubos. *Only One Earth: The Care and Maintenance of a Small Planet.* W. W. Norton & Company, Inc., New York, 1972. Examines environmental problems in a global perspective. Discussed are the social, economic and political dimensions of such issues as: misuse of resources, pollution, population, unbalanced development, and urbanization. Drafted originally as an unofficial report for the United Nations Conference on the Human Environment.

Woodward, G. Vann, ed. *The Comparative Approach to American History.* Basic Books, N.Y., 1968. Using a chronological framework of traditional topics, twenty-two historians attempt to reinterpret the American Revolution, the frontier movement, world wars, and several other topics, within a comparative framework.

Articles

Barnet, Richard. "The Game of Nations." *Harper's,* November 1971. Examines the mentality behind America's belief that in order to be the number one nation you have to be able to do what you want, when and where you want to do it.

Cousins, Norman. "Needed: A New World Theme Song." *Saturday Review,* July 13, 1968. An appeal for a change of emphasis in international and cross-cultural contacts.

Janis, Irving. "Groupthink." *Psychology Today,* November 1971. Argues that the drive for consensus at any cost helps explain foreign policy disasters in Vietnam, Cuba, and Korea.

Smart, Reginald. "The Goals and Definitions of International Education: Agenda for Discussion." *International Studies Quarterly,* December 1971. Identifies several different widely accepted goals for international education and demonstrates the need to face honestly their implications. The goals are: national power, mutual understanding, permeation of ideas, and national development.

Thompson, William Irwin. "Planetary Vistas." *Harper's,* December 1971. Looks toward a transformation of civilization to planetization with a mystical view to guide humankind.

Wright, James D. "Life, Time and the Fortunes of War." *Transaction*, January 1972. The report of a study of whose opinions are more manipulated by the mass media—the common man or the upper-middle class elites.

Pamphlets

Bloomfield, Lincoln P. *The UN and World Order.* Headline Series #197, Foreign Policy Association, New York, October 1969. Examines the UN role in the efforts to create world order in the 1970s.

Brown, Lester. *The Interdependence of Nations.* Headline Series #212, Foreign Policy Association, New York, 1972. An overview of the chief, world-wide threats to human well-being—hunger, environmental deterioration, population growth and the widening rich-poor gap. The author calls for a reordering of global priorities and argues for replacing United States foreign policy with one more sensitive to the increasingly interdependent world.

Howe, James W. *Interdependence and the World Economy.* Headline Series #222, Foreign Policy Association, New York, 1974. An analysis of the impact of oil crises on the global economy. Suggests that the developments in the oil industry herald a new era in which the health and vigor of the international economic order must increasingly become the concern of all nations.

Hutchins, Robert. *The Future of International Relations.* United Nations Institute for Training and Research, 801 United Nations Plaza, New York, 1970. The author argues that nations should think of education as a means to full humanity for their populations rather than as a means to power, prestige, or wealth.

Kenworthy, Leonard. *The International Dimension of Education.* Association for Supervision and Curriculum Development, National Education Association, Washington, D.C. 1970. A report on efforts to incorporate the international dimension of education into the total learning experience of students at all levels; includes practical suggestions for teachers. Available from ERIC; ED 039 202.

Rolfe, Sidney I. *The Multinational Corporation.* Headline Series #199, Foreign Policy Association, New York, February 1970. Examines various facets of the multinational corporation, its economic and political consequences, the political demands it makes, and national responses to it.

Shaw, Robert. *Rethinking Economic Development.* Headline Series #208, Foreign Policy Association, New York, 1971. Outlines a new strategy for economic development emphasizing employment. Examines implications of this focus for the rich countries.

The United Nations: The World as a Developing Country. U.S. Government Printing Office, Washington, D.C., June 1971. A report to the Committee on Foreign Relations, United States Senate. Focuses on the "Seabed" and "Development" issues.

Other Publications

For additional suggestions, see "A Bibliography of International Studies," *Guide to Reading for Social Studies Teachers.* National Council for the Social Studies, Washington, D.C. 20036, 1972.

For a review of the world studies emphasis in a selection of "the new social studies" materials, see *Global Dimensions in the Social Studies* by John H. Spurgin and Gary R. Smith. Center for Teaching International Relations, University of Denver, Denver, Colorado 80210; and Social Science Education Consortium, Inc., 855 Broadway, Boulder, Colorado 80302, 1973.

The following publications contain a wealth of suggested activities, exercises and lessons:

Millar, Jayne C. *Focusing on Global Poverty and Development: A Resource Book for Educators.* Overseas Development Council, Washington, D.C., 1974; *Ideas and Action Bulletin: Action for Development.* Available from FFH/Action for Development, Food and Agriculture Organization, 00100 Rome, Italy.

Global Development Studies, a model curriculum for an academic year course in global systems and human development at the secondary and undergraduate levels of general education. Management Institute for National Development, New York, 1973.

Intercom. Center for War/Peace Studies, New York. See especially, *Teaching Toward Global Perspectives,* #73; *Teaching Global Issues Through Simulation: It Can Be Easy,* #75; *Conflict and Change: Themes for U.S. History,* #76.

See also *Social Education.* November-December 1974, Vol. 38, no. 7, Special Issue—Global Hunger and Poverty.

Selected Sources of Information and Materials for Teachers

(1) *Development Forum* is a monthly newspaper published free of charge by the Centre for Economic and Social Information (CESI), United Nations, Palais des Nations, CH-1211 Geneva 10, Switzerland. It is available in English, French, Spanish, Italian, and German. Areas of interest include: Development Education, Disarmament and Development, Economic Development, Environment, Population, Social Development, and Trade. When ordering *Development Forum,* name, address, country, and organizational affiliation are requested.

(2) *Focus on Asian Studies* is a quarterly newsletter published for $1.00 a year by the Service Center for Teachers of Asian Studies, Association for Asian Studies, Ohio State University, 29 West Woodruff Avenue, Columbus, Ohio 43210. News and information on activities of organizations interested in Asian studies, teaching ideas, and extensive annotated lists of materials and books are included in each issue. *Focus* is an excellent way for a teacher of Asian studies to keep current on what is happening in the field.

(3) *Headline Series* is published quarterly by the Foreign Policy Association, 345 East 46th Street, New York, New York 10017, at a cost of $1.25 per copy. Back copies are also available; over 70 titles are listed in their 1974 catalogue. Included are the U.S.S.R., Eastern Europe, and Western Europe: 17 titles; Asia: 14 titles; Africa, Latin America, the United Nations, and the Middle East with 5 titles each; United States foreign policy problems: 10 titles; and World Problems: 19 titles. These 60-page booklets give concise treatments of the topics covered.

(4) *Ideas and Action Bulletin* is published monthly, except in the summer, by the Coordinator, FFH/Action for Development, FAO, 00100 Rome, Italy. The Freedom from Hunger campaign and Action for Development are joint projects of the United Nations and the Food and Agriculture Organization, a specialized agency of the United Nations. Many of the articles are written by Third World personnel who have been practically involved in development efforts. The *Bulletin* has about 5 or 6 short articles on development projects in various parts of the world in a typical issue. News from the national committees of the FFH campaign and Action for Development committees and discussion of educational materials from both developed and less developed countries are frequently included as well.

(5) *Intercom* is presently published by the Center for War/Peace Studies, three to five times a year. Subscription rates start at 5 issues for $6.00, with bulk rates available from *Intercom,* 218 East 18th Street, New York, New York 10003. Prior to January, 1969, the magazine was published by the Foreign Policy Association,

whose address is given under (3) above. Some 37 titles are available from the FPA. Up to September, 1973, each issue of *Intercom* had several articles on a single topic, with an extensive bibliography and lists of materials available on the subject. In a major change of format, *Intercom* retains the single topic format, but the bibliographic features have been curtailed. Emphasis is placed on practical teaching suggestions and use of materials in the classroom.

(6) *InterCulture News* is a newsletter published free of charge by InterCulture Associates, Incorporated, Box 277, Thompson, Connecticut 06277. InterCulture Associates specializes in the importation of books, records, and artifacts, primarily from Asia and Africa. Filmstrips and slides are also available. The newsletter is essentially a low-key advertising instrument containing editorials on the educational philosophy behind the company and news of its activities and of other organizations with similar interests.

(7) *Newsletter* is published quarterly for $5.00 a year by the Society for Citizen Education in World Affairs. The address of the *Newsletter* is 187 Stanwich Road, Greenwich, Connecticut 06830. The *Newsletter* consists of three parts. The first contains news of non-governmental organizations and activities dealing with world affairs. The second is news of a more personal sort, a "who's who and what are they doing" of world affairs organizations. Lastly, new materials of the major organizations dealing with world affairs are described.

(8) *Progress Report* is published by the Institute for World Order, 11 West 42nd Street, New York, New York 10036. The Institute for World Order was formed recently from the Institute for International Order and its affiliate, the World Law Fund. The *Progress Report* contains news of the Institute, its activities and news and commentary connected with the Institute's interests.

(9) ERIC (Educational Resources Information Center) is a nationwide information system designed to help educators keep up-to-date in their field. ERIC/ChESS, Clearinghouse for Social Studies/Social Science Education, 855 Broadway, Boulder, Colorado 80302, has produced a number of valuable documents in the world studies field. Included are: *Off the African Shelf: An Annotated Bibliography; The Status of World History Instruction in American Secondary Schools; Teaching International Relations; Global Dimensions in the New Social Studies; A Preliminary Review of the Intercultural Dimensions in International/Intercultural Education, Grades K-14.* It also publishes *Keeping Up*, a free newsletter containing announcements of all publications, news items and a selection of abstracted documents.

B. Ideas and Materials for Use in the Classroom

Borg, Kirsten, ed. *USA Foreign Policy*. McDougal, Littell and Company, Evanston, Illinois, 1974. Selected readings presenting facts and realities of diplomacy and foreign policy. Includes selections on "The Nature of American Foreign Policy," "The Cold War," "The Road to World Leadership," and "The Weapons of Propaganda."

Case Studies of Developing Nations. OXFAM Series, 12 booklets. Houghton Mifflin, Boston, 1967. Problems of poor nations and impact of foreign relief efforts on human beings.

Concern: Extremist; Race; Poverty; Revolution. Silver Burdett Co., Morristown, New Jersey, 1970. Dramatically illustrated series of pamphlets. Each deals with a different topic.

Dunstan, Mary Jane, and Patricia W. Garlan. *Worlds in the Making, Probes for Students of the Future*. Prentice-Hall, Englewood Cliffs, New Jersey, 1970. Challenges students to become aware of their values, to seek new meanings in the changing present by exploring, imagining, and evaluating futures. Includes problems, probes, and projections to stimulate the reader and open his or her vision to new possibilities.

Ehrlich, Paul R. and Anne H. Ehrlich. *The End of Affluence: A Blueprint for Your Future.* Ballantine Books, New York, 1974. Describes how the world system is functioning, cites population growth, increasing affluence, and faulty use of technology as major factors in the declining quality of life, and offers suggestions for survival.

Fersh, Seymour, ed. *Learning about Peoples and Cultures.* McDougal, Littell and Company, Evanston, Illinois, 1974. An excellent selection of visuals, readings and commentary dealing with human viewpoints and cultural patterns.

Four Communities Around the World (and Teacher's Guide). The Taba Social Studies Curriculum, Addison-Wesley Publishing Co., Menlo Park, California, 1969. A series of curriculum guides and teaching units, interdisciplinary and planned for sequential development of skills and attitudes as well as knowledge.

Geography in the Urban Age and Teacher's Guide with each of six units. High School Geography Project, School Division, Macmillan and Company, 866 Third Ave., New York, 1969-70. A new approach to the teaching of geography using simulations; topics include "Japan," "Cultural Geography," "Political Processes," and "Habitat and Resources."

"Great Decisions 1975." Foreign Policy Association, New York, 1972. Concise summaries and discussion of questions relating to eight current foreign policy or world issues. Topics include "Japan," "The Soviet Union Today," "The World Food Problem," and "The Oceans and the Seabed."

Hunter, Robert. *Power and Peace.* Overseas Development Council, 1717 Massachusetts Ave., N.W., Washington, D.C., 1973. 20 pp. $.50.

Long, Barbara. *The Road Game.* Herder and Herder, New York, 1970. An interdisciplinary exercise seeking to integrate verbal and visual behavior and designed to help students become better observers of human behavior.

The Value Game. Herder and Herder, New York, 1970. A game designed to reveal differing value systems.

Massialas, Byron G., and Jack Zevin. *World Order.* World Order Through Inquiry Series. Rand McNally, Chicago, 1970. A concept-oriented unit dealing with how conflicts have been and might be handled.

Media Supported World Affairs Seminars. Association of School Librarians, 503 E. Huron, Chicago, 1971. A report on the use of the seminar method in high school classes studying current world affairs issues. Contains actual dialogue. Issues include: "America's Position in China," "Allende Election in Chile," "Arab-Israeli Conflict," and "Detente in Europe."

"Man at Aq Kupruk: Tradition and Change in Village Life," a teaching/learning packet; also *Perspectives* (a set of 12 separate booklets on a single theme). American Universities Field Staff, 3 Lebanon Street, Hanover, New Hampshire 03755. Topics include: "The Impact of Modernization on Traditional Societies," and "The Impact of Population on Society."

Sociological Resources for Secondary School. Allyn and Bacon, Boston, 1970. Based on selected sociological concepts such as culture, stereotypes, ideology, and values. These materials emphasize the process of sociological inquiry. Includes episodes (short units) and readings which can be used to supplement problems of democracy in other social studies courses.

The Concerns of Man. A Literature Series, McDougal, Littell and Company, Evanston, Illinois 60204. Topics include: brotherhood, environment, war, and peace.

Tradition and Change in Four Societies: An Inquiry Approach (and Teacher's Guide). Holt, Rinehart & Winston, New York, 1968. An examination of traditional society, the impact of Western institutions, technology, and selected ideas on South Africa, Brazil, India, and China. Problems studied include race relations and their implications in Brazil and South Africa.

"World Citizenship Declaration." United Nations Association of Minnesota, 55 South 8th Street, Minneapolis, Minnesota 55415; "Declaration of World Citizenship." State of Minnesota, 1971. Printed on parchment suitable for framing.

PART II
Guidelines for World Studies

A. Guidelines and Checklist for World Studies

The guidelines are designed to help you identify goals and priorities in your school or school district. The checklist is to assist you in determining needs and interests and in choosing materials which seem appropriate for your students.

Important	Of some importance	Of little importance	

Guidelines for World Studies

1.0 **The Social Studies Program Should Provide Intercultural Experiences for All Students**

    1.1 All students should have opportunities for intercultural education at all grade levels.

    1.2 The program should provide intensive and recurrent study of cultural, racial, religious, ethnic and national groups, both those to which students themselves belong and those to which they do not.

    1.3 The program should offer opportunities for students to meet, discuss, study, and work with members of various cultural, racial, religious, ethnic and national groups other than their own.

2.0 **The Social Studies Program Should Deal with the Real Global Society**

    2.1 The program should emphasize the major social processes and problems within global society; i.e., intergroup conflict and the control of violence.

    2.2 The program should emphasize current and controversial problems of international society.

    2.3 The program should include both analysis of these problems and attempts to formulate potential solutions.

3.0 **The Social Studies Program Should Draw from Currently Valid Knowledge about Global Society and Humankind's Experience, Culture and Beliefs**

    3.1 The program should emphasize that the planet earth is one of many entities in the larger cosmic system.

    3.2 The program should develop students' understanding of humankind viewed as one species among many forms of life.

    3.3 The program should develop students' understanding of the international social system viewed as one system among many social systems in which they participate.

Guidelines for World Studies (continued)

 3.4 The program should emphasize currently valid concepts, principles and theories in the social sciences.
 3.5 The program should draw upon all the social sciences—not only the history of the United States and the histories of the Western and non-Western worlds, but also anthropology, economics, geography, political science and sociology.
 3.6 The program should draw appropriate material from other related fields, such as psychology, law, communications and the natural sciences.
 3.7 The program should include the study not only of humankind's achievements, but also of those events and policies that are commonly considered contrary to present national goals.

4.0 **The Social Studies Curriculum Should Facilitate the Development of Attitudes and Skills That Students Need to Understand International Society**
 4.1 The program should develop students' ability to adopt a world-centered perspective.
 4.2 The program should develop the capacity of students to consume discriminately and process critically information about their world environment.
 4.3 The program should prepare students intellectually and emotionally to cope with continuous change and marked diversity in their world environment.
 4.4 The program should help students to accept and cope constructively with "the realities of the human condition."

Checklist for World Studies

1.0 **The Social Studies Program Should Provide Intercultural Experiences for All Students**
 1.1 Do all students have ample opportunity for intercultural education at all grade levels?
 1.2 Does the program provide intensive and recurrent study of cultural, racial, religious, ethnic and national groups?
 1.3 Does the program offer opportunities to meet and work with members of racial, cultural, religious, ethnic and national groups other than the students' own?

Checklist for World Studies (*continued*)

2.0 **The Social Studies Program Should Deal with Global Society**

    2.1 Are the following major social processes and problems covered by your program?

        Intergroup conflict and conflict resolution (racial, religious and international)

        Intergroup collaboration (international)

        Intergroup violence

        International trade, foreign aid and foreign investment

        International migration

        International communications

        Formation of in-group/out-group attitudes and images

        Foreign policy decision-making

        Cultural diffusion

        Economic and political development

        Population growth

        World-wide urbanization

        Resource depletion (energy crisis, food shortages)

        Deteriorating human environment

        Racism

        Technological change

        Inequalities in the distribution of basic human requirements (i.e., health, wealth and education)

    2.2 Does your program offer students the opportunity to analyze and formulate potential resolutions of international social problems?

3.0 **The Social Studies Program Should Draw from Currently Valid Knowledge about Global Society and Humankind's Experience, Culture and Beliefs**

    3.1 a. Does your program include a cosmological and geological history of our planet?

        b. Does your program emphasize the major features and characteristics of the planet's contemporary geology and geography?

    3.2 a. Does your program emphasize human diversity as manifested in unique individual behaviors, varied cultural systems and differing social systems such as family systems, political systems, and economic systems?

        b. Does the program emphasize humankind's biological and psychic unity?

Checklist for World Studies (*continued*)

  c. Does the program provide opportunities for comparing the human species with other forms of life including animals and imagined life elsewhere in the universe as portrayed in some of our better science fiction?

  d. Does the program emphasize the major events or transformations in the evolution and cultural development of the species?

3.3 Are the following characteristics of global society emphasized in your program?

  Racially diverse (majority non-white)

  Politically uncentralized

  Multi-linguistic

  Religiously diverse (majority non-Christian and non-Jewish)

  Culturally diverse (characterized by significant variation within and among nations)

  Institutionally diverse (varying political, economic and family systems)

  Generally economically depressed

  Interdependent

  Violent

  Rapidly growing

  Increasingly urbanized

  Increasingly mechanized

3.4 Do the concepts, principles and theories emphasized in your courses' content reflect current developments in the social sciences?

3.5 Are the contributions of history and the various social sciences utilized to create an interdisciplinary curriculum content?

3.6 Does your curriculum provide for contributions from areas which, although outside the formal social studies, furnish understandings about humankind? (i.e., law, psychology, communications and the natural sciences)?

3.7 Does your program include the study not only of humankind's achievements but also of those policies contrary to present national goals?

4.0 The Social Studies Curriculum Should Facilitate the Development of Attitudes and Skills That Students Need to Understand International Society

4.1 a. Does the program offer students the opportunity to transcend ethnocentrism by developing a global perspective?

Checklist for World Studies (continued)

    b. Does the program offer students the opportunity to recognize that some degree of ethnocentric bias and cultural distortion is inherent in all perceptions and beliefs about the world?

    c. Does the program offer students the opportunity to perceive commonalities in the basic needs of culturally diverse individuals?

4.2 a. Does the program offer students the opportunity to think conceptually and comparatively about different societies, about historical and current events and about social processes such as conflict and cooperation?

    b. Do students have the opportunity to formulate and test hypotheses and theories about international phenomena using the methods and skills associated with historical scholarship and social scientific inquiry?

    c. Do students have the opportunity to analyze normative arguments or value claims and the values underlying their own judgments?

    d. Do the students have the opportunity to critically analyze and judge the actions or decisions of organized groups in international society and especially the foreign policy decisions of their own government?

    e. Do students have the opportunity to absorb and critically evaluate information about international developments provided by the mass media and interpersonal communications?

4.3 a. Are students given the opportunity to perceive diversity and change as natural or inevitable features of the human condition?

    b. Are students given the opportunity to judge differences between and changes within social institutions?

    c. Do all students have the opportunity for independent study outside the classroom?

4.4 Does the program offer opportunities for the student to consider the moral and policy implications of humankind's growing interdependence?

B. Guidelines for World Studies: Suggested Topics, Content, and Evaluation of Present Program

Suggested Topics: User's Evaluation
- Important
- Of some importance
- Of little importance

Present Programs: User's Evaluation
- Emphasized
- Some emphasis
- Little or none

I. Intercultural Experiences for All Students at All Grade Levels
  A. Intensive and recurrent *study* of:
    1. cultural groups.
    2. racial groups.
    3. religious groups.
    4. ethnic groups.
    5. national groups.
  B. Opportunities to *meet, discuss,* and *work* with:
    1. cultural groups.
    2. racial groups.
    3. religious groups.
    4. ethnic groups.
    5. national groups.

II. Global Society ("the human species has become interdependent at the global level")
  A. Topics
    1. intergroup conflict and resolution.
    2. communication.
    3. foreign policy decision-making.
    4. cultural diffusion.
    5. population concerns.
    6. urbanization (world-wide).
    7. global environment.
    8. racism.
    9. technological change.
    10. diversity and change.
    11. interdependency.
    12. commonalities among peoples.
    13. need to transcend ethnocentrism.
    14. poor distribution of basic human necessities.

APPENDIX

Suggested Topics: User's Evaluation				Present Programs: User's Evaluation		
Important	Of some importance	Of little importance		Emphasized	Some emphasis	Little or none
			B. Problems			
			1. current.			
			2. controversial.			
			3. analysis.			
			4. solutions.			
			C. Up-to-date knowledge about global society			
			1. planet earth is part of the larger cosmic system.			
			2. humankind is one species among many.			
			3. the international social system is one among many social systems.			
			4. the planet's present geology and geography.			
			5. humankind's biological and psychic unity.			
			6. concepts, theories, and principles of:			
			a. anthropology.			
			b. sociology.			
			c. political science.			
			d. economics.			
			e. geography.			
			7. related subjects.			
			a. law.			
			b. psychology.			
			III. Student Attitudes and Skills			
			A. World-centered perspective			
			B. Knowledge discrimination			
			C. Appreciation of the human condition			
			D. Ability to cope with change and diversity			

C. Guidelines for Selecting World Studies Materials*

Some materials and programs are obviously more appropriate for your situation than others. The criteria (on the opposite page) for evaluating World Studies' materials were prepared to assist educators in the selection of appropriate, high-quality materials—textbooks, films, filmstrips, or tapes—that are globally oriented.

Part I lists seventeen topics considered essential to an understanding of global society and provides a means of evaluating how well and to what extent the materials handle these topics. It also provides a means of rating the emphasis put on particular kinds of skills and attitudes.

Part II enables the evaluation of approach and methodology in terms of student participation required and the feasibility of using the materials in a number of disciplines. Parts I and II of the checklist together are useful in helping a teacher to evaluate new materials and re-evaluate old ones.

---

*These guidelines for selecting World Studies materials were prepared by Robert Anthony, Teacher Associate, Diffusion Project, Social Studies Development Center, 1129 Atwater, Indiana University, Bloomington, Indiana 47401.

Criteria for Evaluating World Studies Materials

Title of materials _____

Producer _____

Producer's address _____

Available from _____

Key: *The materials stress or emphasize*
... to a great extent = 4
... to some extent = 3
... to no extent = 2
unable to judge = 1

Part I. Rationale and Objectives	No. Rating	Part II: Content	No. Rating

A. Global Society, materials stress...
  1. intergroup conflict and resolution
  2. international economics
  3. communications (cross-cultural)
  4. foreign policy decision-making
  5. cultural diffusion
  6. population concerns
  7. urbanization (worldwide)
  8. global environment
  9. racism
  10. technological change
  11. diversity and change
  12. interdependency
  13. commonalities among peoples
  14. need to transcend ethnocentrism
  15. inequitable distribution of basic human necessities
  16. impact of culture on self and human experience
  17. culture and language
B. Development of Ways of Thinking, Communicating, Behaving, materials stress....
  1. awareness of ethnocentric effects on thinking
  2. conceptual thinking
  3. comparative thinking
  4. critical thinking
  5. value analysis
  6. moral and policy implications of globalism
  7. interpersonal trust
  8. motivation to act
  9. affect feelings
		A. Discipline Orientation, materials stress...
		  1. inter-disciplinary approach
		  2. multi-disciplinary approach
		  3. single-discipline
		B. Appropriateness of Content
		C. Provision for Student Participation
		  1. games
		  2. simulations
		  3. role-playing
		  4. panels, debates, small-group discussions
		  5. research and library reports
		  6. involvement with the community
		D. Provision for Evaluation (student, teacher)
		  1. observation
		  2. tests	

Permissions

We are grateful to the publishers for granting us permission to reprint or adapt the following material.

Chapter 2

Pages 11 (Table I), 13 (Table III)
> Adaptation of Table 4 (page 107), Gustov Jahoda, "Development of Scottish Children's Ideas and Attitudes About Other Countries," *Journal of Social Psychology*, 1962, 58, 91-108.

Page 14
> Wallace E. Lambert and Otto Klineberg, *Children's Views of Foreign People*, (New York: Irvington Publishers, 1967), p. 33.

Page 14 (Table IV)
> Adaptation of Table 1 (pages 86-87), Harry Targ, "Children's Developing Orientations to International Politics," *Journal of Peace Research*, II, 1970.

Page 16 (Figure 1 and quote)
> Allen D. Glenn, "Elementary School Children's Trust in Nations and Acceptance of Foreign Children" (paper presented at the Annual Meeting of the National Council for the Social Studies, New York, New York, November 24, 1970).

Page 17 (Table VI)
> Table constructed from data presented in B. K. Beyer and E. P. Hicks, "Images of Africa: A Report On What American Secondary Students Know and Believe About Africa South of the Sahara," Pittsburgh, Carnegie-Mellon University, 1968. (Mimeographed.)

Page 20 (Table VII)
> Adaptation of Table 3, "Changes by Grade of Relative Influence of United States and United Nations in Preventing War," Robert D. Hess and Judith V. Torney, *The Development of Political Attitudes in Children*, (Chicago: Aldine Publishing Company, 1967).

Pages 22 (Table VIII), 25 (Table IX)
> Remmers, H. H., Drucker, A. J., and Shimberg, B., The citizenship attitudes of high school youth. *Report of Poll 22* of the Purdue Opinion Panel,© Purdue Research Foundation, 1949, 8(4).
>
> Remmers, H. H., Horton, R. E., and Mainer, R. E. Does youth believe in the Bill of Rights? *Report of Poll 30* of the Purdue Opinion Panel,© Purdue Research Foundation, 1951, 2(1).
>
> Blumenfeld, W. S., Remmers, H. H., and Weisbrodt, J., Citizenship attitudes of youth: 1949-1963. *Report of Poll 69* of the Purdue Opinion Panel,© Purdue Research Foundation, 1963, 22(3).
>
> Remmers, H. H., Leidy, T. R., Starry, A. R., Shuman, D. L., and Tesser, A. High school students' attitudes on two controversial issues: War in Southeast Asia and the use of personality and ability tests. *Report of Poll 77* of the Purdue Opinion Panel,© Purdue Research Foundation, 1966, 25(3).
>
> Van Horn, C., and Erlick, A. C. The American way of life: Politics, patriotism, isolation. *Report of Poll 90* of the Purdue Opinion Panel,© Purdue Research Foundation, 1971, 30(1).

Page 29
> Trond Alvik, "The Development of Views on Conflict, War and Peace Among School Children: A Norwegian Case Study," *Journal of Peace Research*, V (1968), 171-95.

Pages 30, 31, 32, 38
> Reprinted by permission of the publisher from Howard Tolley, Jr., *Children and War*, (New York: Teachers College Press, copyright 1973 by Teachers College, Columbia University).

Pages 30-31
> Peter Cooper, "The Development of the Concept of War," *Journal of Peace Research*, II (1966), p. 6.

Page 31 (Figure 2)
> Adaptation of Table III.7 (page 45), in Howard Tolley, *Children and War: Political Socialization to International Conflict*, (New York: Teachers College Press, 1973).

Page 32
> Sibylle K. Escalona, "Children's Responses to the Nuclear War Threat," *Children*, X (1963), p. 139.

Page 33 (Figure 3)
> Adaptation from Table IV.2 (page 69), Howard Tolley, *Children and War: Political Socialization to International Conflict*, (New York: Teachers College Press, 1973).

Page 35 (Table XI)
> Adaptation of Table 1 (page 467), Richard C. Remy and James A. Nathan, "The Future of Political Systems: What Young People Think," *Futures*, (December, 1974), Volume 6, Number 6.

Page 36 (Figure 4)
> Adaptation from Figure 2, (page 469), Richard C. Remy and James A. Nathan, "The Future of Political Systems: What Young People Think," *Futures*, (December, 1974), Volume 6, No. 6.

Page 37 (Figure 5)
> Richard C. Remy, "High School Seniors' Attitudes Toward Their Civics and Government Instruction," *Social Education*, (October, 1972), 594.

Page 38
> R. W. Connell, *The Child's Construction of Politics*, (Carlton, Victoria, Australia: Melbourne University Press, 1971) pp. 128-29.

Chapter 3

Page 47
> James MacGregor Burns and Jack W. Peltason, *Government by the People*, (Englewood Cliffs, N. J.: Prentice-Hall, 1969, 7th ed.), p. 500.

Page 48
> Thomas C. Schelling, *Arms and Influence*, (New Haven: Yale University Press, 1966), p. 2.

Page 53
> Reprinted by permission from *Time*, The Weekly Newsmagazine; copyright Time, Inc.

Page 54
> Hans J. Morgethau, *Truth and Power*, (New York: Praeger, Copyright © 1970), p. 291.

Page 55
> R. C. Preston, "World Understanding in the Curriculum," in *Teaching World Understanding*, (Englewood Cliffs: Prentice-Hall, Inc., 1965), p. 108.

Page 55
> W. G. Tyrrell, "Developing International Understanding in the First Two Years of College," in *Approaches to an Understanding of World Affairs*, (Washington, D. C.: National Council for the Social Studies Yearbook, 1954), p. 383.

Page 56
    J. R. Skretting, D. A. Arnold and Robert Weiss, "International Relations," in *Educating Citizens for Democracy*, (New York: Oxford University Press, 1958), p. 323.

Page 58
    William H. Griffin, "The International Component of Citizenship Education," *Social Education*, Vol. XXVII, No. 2, (February 1963), 73-74.

Page 59
    Walter Laves, "The Changing Role of the Nation-State's Imperative Value to Things Beyond the Nation-State," *National Elementary Principal*, Vol. XL, No. 4, (January 1961), 35-38. Copyright 1961, National Association of Elementary School Principals. All rights reserved.

Page 59
    Lee F. Anderson, "An Examination of the Structure and Objectives of International Education," *Social Education*, Vol. XXXIII, No. 7, (November 1968), 645.

Chapter 4

Page 72
    Reginald Smart, "The Goals and Definitions of International Education: Agenda for Discussion," *International Studies Quarterly*, Vol. 15, No. 4, (December, 1971), 442-464. By permission of the publisher, Sage Publications, Inc.

Cover Photo: National Aeronautics and Space Administration
Book Design and Production by *Willadene Price*